CSIOF Bulletin

Issue No. 5

December 2012

CENTRE FOR THE STUDY OF
ISLAM AND OTHER FAITHS

CSIOF Bulletin

No 5. (2012)

ISSN 1836-3490

ISBN 978-0-9870793-3-6

Editor

Peter Riddell

Assistant Editor

Liz Burley

Production and Cover Design

Ho-yuin Chan

Publishing Services

Published by Melbourne School of Theology Press.
Thank you to Mark Durie for his publishing services.

Centre for the Study of Islam and Other Faiths

Melbourne School of Theology
5 Burwood Highway, Wantirna, Victoria 3152, Australia.
PO Box 6257, Vermont Sth, Victoria 3133, Australia
Ph: +61 3 9881 7800, Fax: +61 3 9800 0121
csiof@mst.edu.au, www.mst.edu.au

People involved in the field of Muslim-Christian relations are welcome to submit related items to the Editor for consideration for publishing in the CSIOF Bulletin.

Editorial

In this 2012 issue of the CSIOF Bulletin we have a rich collection of contributions addressing two main themes: Islam and its primary texts and Christian-Muslim relations in the contemporary world.

Bernie Power has provided several stimulating articles that consider fundamental questions for Christians relating to the nature of God and the role of Muhammad. As part of this discussion he asks whether it is even possible to study the tradition of another religion. Christina Cirucci and Brent Neely then consider various angles on the Bible and Qur'an, taking account of both textual and narrative elements.

The second section of feature articles casts a spotlight on diverse contexts in the Islamic world: Malaysia, Indonesia, Afghanistan, Mali and Nigeria. It is difficult to examine such locations without considering the experience of Christians living under Islamic majorities. Andy Bannister gives shape to this issue in his excellent analysis of religious persecutions, its causes and roots.

The Communiqués and reviews provide information on various lectures and related activities at a number of different locations in Australia and overseas, as well as perspectives on several recent books of interests to our readership.

We hope that you enjoy reading this year's issue of the CSIOF Bulletin.

Features

Do we Worship the Same God?

Dr Bernie Power

Lecturer, CSIOF, MST

A Muslim student stood to his feet. "Can't you just agree with us that we all worship the same God?," he asked, to much applause.

The event, "What is at the heart of Islam/Christianity?" at Melbourne University late last year had been organised by the Christian Union and the Muslim Students Association, where I was invited to compare the Muslim and Christian views of God.

At one point, I quoted the famous Muslim theologian, al Ghazali, who wrote: "Love is to sense a need of the beloved and since Allah cannot be said to have a need or an experience of a need, it is therefore impossible that Allah should love". This contrasts with a key verse in the Bible (John.3:16), and the statement that "God is love" (1.Jn.4:8,16). The Muslim speaker responded vigorously, challenging the authenticity of the Bible and holding up his Qur'an as "the only true and unchanged word of God". Some Muslims in the audience called out loudly: "Allah Akbar" (Allah is great). The lines were drawn and the atmosphere was tense.

"Do we worship the same God?" I responded, "Let's test that."

"Could I ask all the Muslim students to raise their hands? I am going to say something, and if you hear anything you disagree with, please put your hand down." I began to recite the Apostles' Creed: "I believe in God, the Father almighty, Creator of heaven and earth." At the word "Father", some hands went down.

I continued: "And in Jesus Christ, His only Son, our Lord." Most hands dropped after this, but crept up momentarily as I said: "He was conceived by the Holy Spirit, born of the Virgin Mary, suffered under Pontius Pilate, was crucified, died and was buried." At this point every hand in the room went down. I turned to the questioner: "Look around, and you will see that not a single Muslim agrees with this early creed that almost every Christian accepts. How can you say that we worship the same God?" There was silence, and the meeting moved on to another topic.

Other Christians, such as Miroslav Volf, would take a different approach. They point to the linguistic similarities between the Hebrew 'Eloah' and 'Elohim', and the Arabic 'Allah'. The Aramaic term that Jesus would have used for God was 'Aalah'. The Qur'an claims that Muslims and Christians worship the same God (Q.29:46). The Torah (Dt.6:4), Jesus (Mk.12:29) and the Qur'an (Q.112:1) agree that there is only one God. He creates, reveals, loves, forgives, and judges. Surely, according to Muslims and some Christians, this must be the same God.

However a closer inspection reveals some significant differences in the way these actions are carried out. In the Bible, God reveals Himself as personal, for people can know God (Jer.31:34), most supremely through Christ (Jn.17:3). But the Islamic understanding is different. Muslim theologian Isma'il al Faruqi states of Allah: "He does *not* reveal Himself. He does not reveal Himself to anyone in any way. God reveals only His will."

The Bible proclaims God's love for all, including sinners (Romans.5:8). The Qur'an is less accepting. The nineteen references to those whom Allah loves include "the doers of good", the "pious" and "equitable" people. The twenty-eight references to those whom Allah does **not** love include "sinners", "transgressors" and "evil-doers". Allah's love is contingent on the recipient's prior behaviour. Daud Rahbar noted that "unqualified Divine love for mankind is an idea completely alien to the Qur'an... nowhere do we find the idea that God loves mankind. God's love is conditional." [Rahbar later became a Christian.]

According to the Qur'an, Allah forgives, but a frequent refrain is that "he forgives whom he wills, and punishes whom he wills" (e.g. Q.2:284) Allah's determination is supreme, for many times it is stated that "Allah sends astray whom He wills and He guides on the Straight Path whom He wills." (e.g. Q.6:39) This is a far cry from the biblical representation of the God who "is patient with you, not wanting anyone to perish, but everyone to come to repentance." (2.Pet.3:9) He calls out agonisingly to people: "I take no pleasure in the death of the wicked, but rather that they turn from their ways and live. Turn! Turn from your evil ways! Why will you die?" (Ezek.33:11).

God's forgiveness in the Bible is based on the death of Christ and it is here that the greatest gulf exists between Islam and Christianity. The Qur'an denies the death of Christ, claiming that he was not crucified but taken up alive to heaven (Q.4:157).

The identity of Jesus is altered. He was "nothing but a prophet" (Q.5:75) and clearly not the Son of God (Q.9:30), for Allah does not have a son (Q.4:171). Allah is never described as 'Father' in the Qur'an. It gives a distorted view of the Trinity, consisting of God, Mary and Jesus (Q. 5:73, 116). The term "Holy Spirit" refers to the angel Gabriel (Q.16:102). There is a clear dissonance.

Imagine two old school friends discussing a former fellow-student named Theo. One insists that Theo was tall and muscular, the captain of the football team, but the other that Theo was short and fat, a member of the debating team. The characteristics are not lining up. A check of the yearbook photos shows that they are talking about two different Theos (bad pun intended!). An identical name and some shared characteristics (both Theos attended the same school) does not always indicate the same person. The Australian man "Bernie Power", according to an internet search, is a Queensland multi-millionaire made rich by the brewing business – but he is not me!

As the Bible and the Qur'an describe God, there appears to be little agreement on the critical characteristics. The Bible tells of a Triune God – Father, Son and Holy Spirit (Mt.28:19). The Father, out of love for the world, sends His Son. Jesus is born, lives a perfect life and dies as a sacrifice for the sins of humanity. After Christ's resurrection, the Holy Spirit comes to dwell in those who believe in Christ. The Qur'an, however, denies the orthodox Christian Trinity, and rejects the divine Sonship, incarnation, death and resurrection of Christ. It presents Allah as an undifferentiated monad, a somewhat disengaged, unknowable and capricious being. It seems inconceivable that the God of the Bible and Allah of the Qur'an are the same God.

"What do you think of Muhammad?" [1]

Dr Bernie Power

It was clearly a set-up. I'd been invited to the house of a neighbour for dinner. We had been living in this Middle Eastern country for several years and it was well-known that I was an active Christian. When I walked into his sitting-room, there were about 20 men from the local mosque, reclining on the mattress-type cushions placed against the walls. The only spare seat was beside the bearded *imam* at the far end of the long room. I had often listened to his fiery sermons broadcast through the public loudspeakers into our neighbourhood. He motioned me to sit down beside him. He then gave a little sermon for me on the benefits of Islam and invited me to submit to Allah. Through stories, I explained how Christ had saved me and fulfilled all my needs.

"But what about Muhammad? What do you think of him?" he asked. "We accept Christ as a prophet, why don't you accept Muhammad?"

Every one leaned forward. They wanted to know what this foreigner thought. "The answer is simple," I said. "Imagine you are going somewhere you haven't been to before. You come to a fork in the road. You are unsure which way to go. Fortunately there are two people at the crossroads. One of them has been before to the place you are going to, and he is alive. The other one has never been there, and he is dead. Who will you ask: the live person, or the dead one?" Everyone leaned backwards. The analogy was obvious: Muslims know that Muhammad is dead and buried in Medina. They also believe that Jesus never died, but was taken up alive to heaven, and he will return in the last days.

The *imam* continued. "Even though Muhammad is dead, he was still a prophet, a messenger from God." I nodded. "Yes, you believe that, but I don't, otherwise I would be a Muslim. But what I think

---

[1] Published in *Working Together* (Magazine of the Australian Evangelical Alliance Inc), 2006 Issue 2 p.5

about Muhammad is not important. I am just a man like you, with my own opinions. The more important question is: What did Muhammad claim for himself? In the Qur'an he says to his followers: 'I am no innovation among the prophets, and I do not know what will happen to me or what will happen to you.' (Surah 46:9). Muhammad, as great a man as he was, did not know whether he would enter paradise or not. Whereas Jesus says: 'I am the way, the truth, and the life, no-one to the Father except by me' (Jn.14:6). Muhammad claimed to bring nothing new, and Jesus came to open the gate to heaven."

The widespread frowns showed me that this idea was not accepted. The *imam* spoke for them all: "No, everyone must get to heaven by their works. No-one can be the mediator for anyone else (Surah.74:48)."

"That's interesting," I replied, "because I have been reading the *Hadith*, the sayings of the prophet recorded by his companions. One day Muhammad said: "The good deeds of any person will not make him enter Paradise." (i.e. none can enter Paradise through his good deeds.) The Prophet's companions said, "Not even you, O Allah's Apostle?" He said, "Not even myself, unless Allah bestows His favour and mercy *(rahma)* on me." (Hadith al-Bukhari 7:577)." This saying was well known, because several of the listeners recited the last sentence along with me in Arabic. I continued: "And who, according to the Qur'an, is the mercy *(rahma)* of God? It is one of the titles of Jesus (Surah.19:20/21). Just like Muhammad, each one of us needs Jesus, the mercy of God, in order to be saved. There is no other way. God is one, and the path of salvation is one." There was a silence and they moved onto another topic.

At the end of the evening, I rose and went around the room, shaking hands and kissing everyone, as is the local custom. I asked their forgiveness if I had offended anyone, which they all assured me was not the case. Afterwards, one of the men came and asked if I could give him an audiotape of the Gospel, since I had given one to the host of this meeting on a previous occasion. Pray for the seed to fall on fertile ground.

Is it possible to study the tradition of another religion?

Dr Bernie Power

In a critical moment in the important documentary 'Islam – the Untold Story' shown in September 2012 on Channel 4 in the UK, historian Dr Tom Holland asks a pointed question of Seyyed Hossain Nasr, Professor of Islamic Studies at George Washington University. "Can some-one like myself who is not a Muslim and who does not believe that God spoke to Muhammad ever hope to fathom the truth of the origins of Islam?" Nasr responds with a decisive, unequivocal 'No".[1] Yet a Saudi-funded English translation of the Qur'an, being distributed free around the world, contains a ten page appendix attacking standard Christian doctrines.[2] As Islam and Christianity move into closer proximity due to globalization and widespread Muslim immigration to the West, the eyes of their followers inevitably turn on each other with greater intensity. But does anyone have the right to subject the belief system of others to intense and even critical scrutiny? There have been a variety of responses to this question.

a)   Negative responses from non-Muslims

Some Westerners would immediately give a negative response, claiming that such a venture is fraught with danger from the start. They are wary of interacting with writings of other cultures and traditions at this level. "By the very act of engaging in cross-cultural research, the Western scholar has automatically imposed his own values into his transaction with his subjects, and if he wishes to go through with the exercise, they must accept the element of

---

[1] This one hour documentary was available in 2 parts on http://rutube.ru/embed/5841352 & http://rutube.ru/embed/5841504 in October 2012, but the site has since been corrupted. For discussion of this documentary by US commentator Michael Coren, see http://www.youtube.com/watch?v=ViaSttOj8E4

[2] Muhammad Taqi-ud-din al-Hilali & Muhammad Muhsin Khan *Translation and meanings of the Noble Qur'an in the English Language* (Madinah, KSA: King Fahd Complex, 1430 A.H.) pp.907-917

ethnocentrism that is inherent in this."[3] Any religious system can be approached from either an *emic* or *etic* perspective.[4] *Emic* is an 'insider' stance. It presupposes that the community to be addressed has a worldview which they believe to be consistent and real. An *emic* approach takes this seriously, seeking to ascertain the nodes and linkages which hold this worldview together.[5]

One Catholic priest sees any assessment by a non-Muslim as doomed to failure. Outlining his objective of describing Islam in terms acceptable to Muslims, Renard comments: "Obviously no outsider can portray an insider's truth in an altogether unbiased fashion."[6] Edward Said, a Palestinian Christian, suggested that most Western study of the East is at best patronising, and at worst, a form of imperialism. He refers to it as 'Orientalism', a myopic academic approach which stereotypes Easterners and Eastern cultures, treating them as objects of study. He claims: "… because of Orientalism the Orient was not (and is not) a free subject of thought or action."[7] Even more dismissive was his comment that "every European, in what he could say about the Orient, was … a racist, an imperialist and almost totally ethnocentric".[8]

It is a moot point whether *any* person, insider or not, can be totally objective. Einstein perceptively noted: "Whether you can observe a thing or not depends on the theory which you use. It is the theory which decides what can be observed."[9] Every individual carries some predispositions based on his or her worldview, culture, upbringing and personal experience. At the very least, it may involve familiarity with and acceptance of the thought-forms and practices of another culture, whereby they are presented in a neutral

---

[3] Taft "Cross-cultural psychology as a social science" (1976) quoted in Geert Hofstede *Culture's Consequences* (Thousand Oaks, CA: Sage, 2001 (2nd ed), 19

[4] This distinction was proposed by Kenneth Pike in *Language in relation to a unified theory of structure of human behaviour* (The Hague: Mouton, 1967 [2nd edition])

[5] Russell McCutcheon (ed.) *The Insider/Outsider Problem in the Study of Religion: A Reader* (London: Cassell, 1999)

[6] John Renard *In the footsteps of Muhammad: Understanding the Islamic Experience* (New York: Paulist Press, 1992), 2. These issues are further discussed in Sharpe, Eric *Understanding Religion* (London: Duckworth, 1983), 19ff, and Russell McCutcheon (ed.) *The Insider/Outsider Problem in the Study of Religion: A Reader* (London: Cassell, 1999)

[7] Edward Said *Orientalism* (London: Penguin, 1978, reprinted 2003), 3. A critical response to Said has been given by the Ibn Warraq website 2006.

[8] Edward Said *Orientalism* (London: Routledge and Kegan Paul, 1978), pp.203-4

[9] quoted in Abdus Salam *Unification of Fundamental Forces* (Cambridge: Cambridge University Press, 1990), 81

manner, as 'normal'. At worst, people hold biases and prejudices against certain ideas or types of behaviour. Such negative assumptions will result in a distorted perception and representation of the other culture.

b)   Negative responses from Muslims

There is also resistance from within the Islamic community towards analysis by outsiders, as we saw in the exchange between Holland and Nasr above. From its earliest days Islam did not always welcome independent enquiry and evaluation of its sacred texts. Muhammad forbade his followers from carrying copies of the Qur'an into hostile countries (al-Bukhari 4:233). The early "Covenant of 'Umar" barred the subjugated Jewish and Christian populations from teaching the Qur'an to their children.[10] "The suspicion that teaching the Qur'an to those who have not accepted Islam will prove destructive is at least one of the subtexts of such statements."[11] A Muslim writer proposed that "a non-Muslim cannot and should not approach a text that means so much to so many people. To do so will surely misrepresent it and will be unacceptable to non-Muslims."[12] A.L. Tibawi postulates that only those who are believers themselves have the right to critique a book of faith. Anyone else should, due to their bias, leave it alone.[13] The test of 'insider' acceptance is applied by al-Faruqi: "No statement about a religion is valid unless it can be acknowledged by that religion's believers."[14] Parvez Manzoor suspects some scholars of being anti-religious and anti-Islamic.[15] The question of the

---

[10] Source: http://www.fordham.edu/halsall/source/pact-umar.html accessed on 7th March, 2008. Also Mark Durie "The Pact of 'Umar" in David Claydon (ed.) *Islam: Human Rights and Public Policy* (Melbourne: Acorn Press, 2009), 37

[11] Andrew Rippin "Western scholarship and the Qur'an" in Jane Dammen McAuliffe (ed.) *The Cambridge Companion to the Qur'an* (Cambridge: Cambridge University Press, 2006), 236

[12] M. Abdul-Rauf "'Outsiders' interpretations of Islam: a Muslim's point of view" in R.C.Martin (ed.) *Approaches to Islam in religious studies* (Tucson: University of Arizona Press, 1985), pp.179-88 cited in Andrew Rippin "Western scholarship and the Qur'an" in Jane Dammen McAuliffe (ed.) *The Cambridge Companion to the Qur'an* (Cambridge: Cambridge University Press, 2006), 245

[13] Tibawi, A. L. "Second Critique of English-Speaking Orientalists and their Approach to Islam and the Arabs," *Islamic Quarterly*, 1979, pp.3-54 pp.5-8).

[14] Isma'il al-Faruqi cited in Ataullah Siddiqui *Christian-Muslim Dialogue in the Twentieth Century* (London: St Martin's Press, 1997), 88

[15] Parvez Manzoor "Method against truth: Orientalism and qur'anic studies" *Muslim World Book Review* 7 (1987), pp.33-49 cited in Andrew Rippin "Western scholarship and the Qur'an" in Jane Dammen McAuliffe (ed.) *The Cambridge Companion to the Qur'an* (Cambridge: Cambridge University Press, 2006), 245

objectivity of non-Muslims is negatively answered by one commentator: "The questions as to whether a disbeliever *(kafir)* is qualified to be recipient and carrier of hadith is answered in the affirmative provided that he is a Muslim when he transmits the hadith to others. A *kafir* is thus qualified to receive hadith but not to transmit it. To accept hadith transmitted by a disbeliever would mean that Muslims are bound by his report that consequently becomes a part of their religion, which is unacceptable."

Former Muslims, such as Salman Rushdie, Ibn Warraq, Taslima Nasrin and Ayaan Hirsi Ali would have all been considered 'insiders' to Islam at some stage, but they now hold a negative view of Islam. This raises the question: At what point does an insider become an outsider? When Mustafa Kemal Attaturk, the founder of modern Turkey, referred to Islam as "the symbol of obscurantism .. a purified corpse which poisons our lives ... the enemy of civilisation and science", [16] was he speaking as an insider or an outsider? More recently, Pakistan's then President Pervez Musharraf announced to his fellow Muslims: "Today we are the poorest, the most illiterate, the most backward, the most unhealthy, the most un-enlightened, the most deprived, and the weakest of all the human race."[17] Did he simply speak the truth based on social and economic indicators, or had he moved beyond the pale of Islam?

On the other hand, some non-Muslims such as Karen Armstrong and John Esposito, write positively of Muhammad and Islam. Will they always be considered 'outsiders'?

For some Muslims, a positive attitude towards Islam is not sufficient. One notes that "as a Muslim, I am naturally sensitive to attempts by others to define what I or my community believes. Few Jews or Christians would delegate to others the definition of themselves or their private and collective devotion."[18] Ghorab is more forthright: "Muslims may not learn Islam from non-Muslims. How should believers receive Islam from those who not only disbelieve in Islam but are hostile to it?"[19] He cites the Qur'anic

---

[16] Quoted in S.Sayyid *A Fundamental Fear* (London: Zed books, 2003), 65

[17] Source: http://news.bbc.co.uk/1/hi/world/south_asia/1824455.stm Accessed on 25th Feb, 2008

[18] Abd-Allah, Umar F. "Do Christians and Muslims Worship the Same God?" Part Five in *The Christian Century*, August 24, 2004, pp. 34-36

[19] Ahmad Ghorab *Subverting Islam: The Role of Orientalist Centres* (Middlesex: Minerva, 1995), 14,75,76

warnings against the Jews and Christians (Q.2:109, 120). One commentator questions the motives of any scholar who reads the Qur'an and does not submit to Islam. "[O]nly the writings of a practicing Muslim are worthy of our attention...[Orientalists] must see Muhammad as a deluded madman or a liar bearing false claims of prophethood ... If they did not set out to prove Muhammad's dishonesty or the Qur'an's fallacy, what would hinder them from accepting Islam?"[20]

Of course, the claim by some that only fellow-Muslims can interpret Islam would be more convincing if there existed and all Muslims agreed with each other on a single interpretation of Islam. Zebiri points out that "the assumption that the adherents of a given tradition are uniquely qualified to understand and interpret it is problematic in view of the diversity within each tradition."[21] Islam itself is not univocal. There are clear differences in interpretation of the Qur'an between Sunnis and Shias, let alone the even greater divergences with groups like the mystic Sufis and unorthodox Ahmadiyya.

c)   A positive response from non-Muslims

The pessimistic view towards the study of other traditions has not always held sway. Abraham Geiger in *Judaism and Islam* (1833) put forward the thesis that "religion in its various manifestations is a product of historical and social forces ..[it is] the result of an initial religious revelation which is subject to human development. As such a sympathetic approach to Islam was called for, one that did not raise the issue of its truth value, one that did not conceive of Muhammad as an 'imposter' or false prophet, but rather one that saw the Prophet within the context of his time."[22] Some propose the goal in assessing another faith system should be grateful acceptance by those who subscribe to that system. Wilfred Cantwell Smith believed "that the aim of an outside scholar writing about Islam is to elicit Muslim approval."[23]

---

[20] Muhammad al-A'zami *The history of the Qur'anic text: From revelation to compilation: A comparative study with the Old and New Testaments* (Leicester: UK Islamic Academy, 2003), 341 cited in Stefan Wild "Political interpretation of the Qur'an" in Jane Dammen McAuliffe (ed.) *The Cambridge Companion to the Qur'an* (Cambridge: Cambridge University Press, 2006), 277

[21] Kate Zebiri *Muslims and Christians Face to Face* (Eugene, OR: Wipf & Stock, 1997), 12

[22] Andrew Rippin "Western scholarship and the Qur'an" in Jane Dammen McAuliffe (ed.) *The Cambridge Companion to the Qur'an* (Cambridge: Cambridge University Press, 2006), 240

[23] quoted in Clinton Bennett *In Search of Muhammad* (London: Cassell, 1998), 7

This view, it could be argued, could only arise in the culturally-sensitive, politically-correct post-modern West. However, Christian writers have sometimes practiced self-censorship when writing about Islam, or when editing the writings of other Christians about Islam. Sir William Muir in his 1887 translation of the ninth century AD *The Apology of Al-Kindy* included the following comment in a footnote: "There are several passages which must be omitted here. Page 98, last eight lines; the reason assigned for circumcision is both childish and indelicate. Page 100, first five lines may be true, but the mode of expression is gross and offensive. Page 102, lower half (and by consequence first seven lines of page 103), relating to Hagar, and a practice current among the Arabs (*Life of Mahomet*, 1st edition, vol. ii. p. 108 note), is at once silly and grossly improper. It is strange that a man of refinement should have admitted such a passage into his book."[24]   W. Montgomery Watt appeared to be ahead of his time in the way he modified Bell's writings: "With the greatly increased contacts between Muslims and Christians during the last quarter of a century, it has become imperative for a Christian scholar not to offend Muslim readers gratuitously, but as far as possible to present his arguments in a form acceptable to them. Courtesy and an eirenic outlook certainly now demand that we should not speak of the Qur'an as the product of Muhammad's conscious mind; but I hold that the same demand is also made by sound scholarship. I have therefore altered or eliminated all expressions which implied that Muhammad was the author of the Qur'an, including those which spoke of his 'sources' or of the 'influences' on him." [25] In other civilizations and at different times, it has been allowed and expected that scholars could study and critically evaluate belief systems different from their own, and that their assessments should be taken seriously. Ironically, the current 'political-correctness' in the West has sometimes become a straitjacket that may inhibit rather than encourage open and free enquiry.

After criticizing the style of the Qur'an, Rodinson feels the need to apologise for any possible offence that he may have caused, while still maintaining his stance. "May any Muslims who happen to read

---

[24] Sir William Muir *The Apology of Al Kindy written at the court of Al Mamun (circa A.H. 215; A.D, 830) in defence of Christianity against Islam* (London: SPCK, 1887), 91 fn 1 from http://www.answering-islam.org/Books/Al-Kindi/p090-091.htm cited on 18th March, 2009

[25] Montgomery Watt, *Bell's Introduction to the Quran* (Edinburgh: Edinburgh University Press, 1970), introduction

these lines forgive my plain speaking. For them the Koran is the book of Allah and I respect their faith. But I do not share it and I do not wish to fall back, as many orientalists have done, on equivocal phrases to disguise my meaning. This may perhaps be of assistance in remaining on good terms with individuals and governments professing Islam; but I have no wish to deceive anyone. Muslims have every right not to read the book or to acquaint themselves with the ideas of a non-Muslim, but if they do so, they must expect to find things put forward there which are blasphemous to them. It is evident that I do not believe that the Koran is the book of Allah. If I did I should be a Muslim. But the Koran is there, and since I, like many other non-Muslims, have interested myself in the study of it, I am naturally bound to express my views."[26]

The 'insider' perspective is not the only legitimate one, for an *emic* attitude might suffer from tunnel-vision, finding itself unable or unwilling to consider valid insights from those outside their community. It is true that an undiscerning *etic* (outsider) approach may not recognize the needs, strengths and contributions of the focus culture, and simply impose its own agenda on the situation. Consequently it could be seen as irrelevant. However an outsider may have the advantage of seeing the culture with new eyes, and discerning 'the wood from the trees'. This is something that those wrapped up in their own culture may not be able to clearly see due to 'the log which is in their own eyes' (Mt.7:3).[27] Margoliouth comments: "[A]n outsider who is free from bias is less likely than an adherent to misrepresent the doctrines contained in the sacred book or books of a community. He is immune from the temptation to harmonise inconsistencies and explain away what might shock or offend. And these are temptations to which an adherent, who is apt to be an apologist, frequently succumbs"[28] Albert Hourani, who was much admired by Said, sounded a similar warning regarding *Orientalism*: "I think all this talk after Edward's book also has a certain danger. There is a certain counter-attack of Muslims, who say nobody understands Islam except themselves."[29]

---

[26] Maxime Rodinson *Mohammed* (London: Pelican, 1971), 218

[27] Rudyard Kipling asks rhetorically: "What should they know of England who only England know? *The English Flag*, Stanza 1 (1891) cited in http://www.daypoems.net/poems/1821.html accessed 16th Sept, 2010

[28] David Margoliouth *Mohammed* (London : Blackie & Son, 1939), vi

[29] Source: http://www.secularislam.org/articles/debunking.htm accessed on 18th Sept, 2006

Another Arab writer looks at a broader perspective. Fouad Accad developed a comprehensive exposition of the Gospel by using the Qur'an. He notes: "When some of the Muslims object, saying: 'But what authority do you have from the Muslim leaders permitting you to make such interpretation of our Book?' I answer: 'Was it valid for the early Christians to apply Old Testament Messianic prophecies to Jesus of Nazareth, as we see in the New Testament, without first receiving permission from Jewish leaders?' Understanding and personal application of such material is a common heritage of all humanity."[30]

d) Positive encouragements from within Islam

There is some support from the Qur'an to interact with it. Rather than being a book to be read by the elect only, the Qur'an invites non-believers to investigate its claims. The Qur'an was born in a polemical climate, and it assumes an audience of unbelievers. They are an important backdrop to the text, for 332 verses begin with the command *'qul'* "Say:" (e.g. Q.114:1) indicating that Allah was coaching Muhammad in how to respond to the questions and comments of non-Muslims. The pagans are called upon to bring their own Book (Q.28:49; 37:157), or to at least produce a Sura like the Qur'an (Q.2:23; 10:38), or ten suras (Q.11:13). This is presented as a feat beyond all humans and jinn (17:88). Readers are challenged to find contradictions in its text (Q.4:82). The Qur'an presents itself as a book grounded in truth (Q. 32:3; 35:31; 69:51). Birt insightfully comments: "One need not be a believer to have cognition of historical values."[31]

It would be strange if others would not be allowed to comment on Islam since the Qur'an mentions Christians and Jews, sometimes in positive (e.g. Q.5:82; 57:27) but often in negative ways[32] (Q.3:110; 98:6). The ideas and worldview of Meccan animism are held up to ridicule (c.f. Q.21:51-68 – Abraham's attack on idols), much as the Old Testament prophets did with idolatry (e.g.Isa.44:9-20). Those

---

[30] Fouad Accad *Building Bridges: Christianity and Islam* (Colorado Springs: Navpress, 1997), 16. Such an approach has been criticised by Schlorff, Samuel P. "The hermeneutical crisis in Muslim evangelization" in *Evangelical Missionary Quarterly* (July 1980) Vol. 16, No. 3

[31] M Yahya Birt "The Message of Fazlur Rahman"
http://www.freerepublic.com/focus/fr/531762/posts accessed on 26th March, 2009

[32] Sayyid Qutb disavows any attempt to use Western approaches in preaching and promoting Islam. He maintains that it is very important not to demean Islam by "searching for resemblances" between Islam and the "filth" and "the rubbish heap of the West." *Milestones* (Cairo: Kazi publications, 1964), 139

who do not believe in Islam are slated as enemies deserving attack, and subject to tribute payment and degradation (e.g. Q.9:29).

Islam takes a supercessionist view towards the previous scriptures. Jesus is radically re-interpreted to become a Muslim prophet. Words are put into the mouth of Christ, foretelling the coming of a certain Ahmad (Q.61:6), claimed in the Hadith to be another name for Muhammad (al-Bukahri 6:419). Muhammad, in a dream, sees Jesus performing the *tawaf* (circumabulation) around the Ka'ba (al-Bukhari 4:649, 650; 7:521). During his ascent to heaven, Muhammad meets Jesus and John the Baptist in the second heaven (al-Bukhari 4:429, 640; 5:227), a lower position than many of the other prophets. On his return, it is declared that Jesus will break the cross and kill the pig (al-Bukhari 3:425, 656; 4:657). When believers come to Jesus on the day of resurrection, seeking his intercession, he counsels them: "I am not fit for this undertaking, go to Muhammad the Slave of Allah whose past and future sins were forgiven by Allah." (al-Bukhari 6:3; 8:570; 9:532.3 c.f. 6:236; 9:601). Muslim writers go further, finding prophecies relating to Muhammad and Islam in many places in the Bible.[33]

Seeking a middle course, Arkoun calls for "a protocol of interpretation that is free from both the dogmatic orthodox framework and the procedural disciplines of modern scientism which is, it must be admitted, no less constraining".[34] Al-Faruqi is one among Muslims who "believe it is both possible and desirable to exercise 'epoche', or the 'putting in brackets' of one's own beliefs, when studying another's faith."[35] Many Muslims do, of course, comment on and criticise Christianity, and they should not be surprised when Christian scholars reciprocate.

Conclusion:

This study raised the question whether anyone can authoritatively comment on the teachings of another religion. Its denial, if applied in every situation, could spell the end of all independent

---

[33] Kais al-Kalby *Prophet Muhammad: the last Messenger in the Bible* (Bakersfield, CA: American Muslim Cultural Association, 1991), pp. 159-560 . Remarkable claims to prophecy fulfillment include "Prophet Muhammad baptize (sic.) all the nations with the Holy Spirit" (Mt.3:2-12) and "Calipha Omar rides a donkey to Jerusalem" (Zech.9:9-10).

[34] M. Arkoun "Contemporary critical practices and the Qur'an" in Jane Dammen McAuliffe (ed.) *Encyclopaedia of the Qur'an*, 5 vols (Leiden: Brill, 2001-6), Vol.1 pp.412-31

[35] Ismail al-Faruqi *Christian Ethics* pp.3-8 summarised in Kate Zebiri *Muslims and Christians Face to Face* (Eugene, OR: Wipf & Stock, 1997), 149

scholarship: only co-religionists could comment on their own tradition. The Qur'an's comments on Judaism and Christianity would likewise be rendered invalid. The result is a complete *reductio ad absurdum.*

While it is true that only the adherents of a particular religion should be allowed to *define* that religion, and determine its beliefs and practices, it does not follow that they alone should be allowed to comment on and assess it. Religions, like all communal organizations, should be open for evaluation by all. Closing down public comment on any institution is an indication of totalitarianism which seeks to limit the free and open discourse of a particular belief system.

The Challenge of the Sana'a Manuscripts to the Muslim Claim of the Perfect Qur'an

Christina A. Cirucci M.D.

Student in Biblical Studies
Columbia International University, Columbia, SC

Muslims believe that the Qur'an is the perfectly maintained record of the exact words of God as revealed to the Prophet Muhammad between 610 and 632 AD. In contradistinction to the Christian view of the Bible (that the Bible is the Word of God, inerrant in its *original* form), Muslims believe that the Qur'an is inerrant in its *current* form. Until recently, the oldest Qur'an manuscripts were dated not earlier than one hundred years after Muhammad's death or 732 AD.[1,2] In 1972, however, Qur'an manuscripts were found at a mosque in Sana'a, Yemen. The oldest of these manuscripts have been dated between 700 and 715 AD.[3] There are differences in the oldest Sana'a Qur'an and the Qur'an that is in use today, and although the differences do not change the principal meaning, the find is a challenge to the Muslim view that the Qur'an has been maintained exactly as it was given to Muhammad 1400 years ago.

In 1972, ancient parchments comprised of tens of thousands of fragments from almost a thousand different parchment codices of the Qur'an[4] were discovered during restoration of the Great Mosque in Sana'a, Yemen. The parchments were locked up until 1979 when Qadhi Ismail al-Akwa', the president of the Yemeni Antiquities Authority, recruited German scholar Dr. Gerd Puin to preserve and examine the documents. Puin was later joined by his

---

[1] John Gilchrist, *Jam'al-Quran: The Codification of the Qur'an Text* (Mondeor, South Africa: MERCSA, 1989) http://www.answering-islam.org/Gilchrist/Jam/chap7.html (accessed August 18, 2011)

[2] Ahmad Von Denffer, *Ulum al-Quran: An Introduction to the Sciences of the Qur'an* (Leicestershire, UK: The Islamic Foundation, 2007), 61.

[3] Gerd Puin, as quoted in "The Oldest Qur'anic Manuscripts" http://www.youtube.com/watch?v=iNdvsLh128Q (accessed August 9, 2011)

[4] Toby Lester. "What is the Koran?" *The Atlantic Monthly*, January 1999, http://www.theatlantic.com/issues/99jan/koran.htm.

colleague from Saarland University, Hans-Caspar Graf von Bothmer. Although the Germans have since been denied further access to the original manuscripts, there is a complete microfilm copy in Germany. The account of the Sana'a manuscripts is well documented in Toby Lester's article, "What is the Koran?" published in the January 1999 issue of *The Atlantic Monthly*.[5]

The Sana'a manuscripts are likely older than any other extant Qur'an manuscripts. Four fragments containing the first and last chapters of the Qur'an contain architectural drawings of mosques which allows for precise dating of the manuscripts. Puin states, "Because of its drawings, because of the art-historical context, you can date this Qur'an very precisely to the time of Al-Walid. This is the reign between 705 and 715."[6] Carbon 14 testing dates some of the manuscripts to 645-690 AD.[7]

Puin claims that the Sana'a manuscripts contain differences compared to today's Qur'an consisting of different verse orderings, minor textual variants, and rare styles of orthography and artistic embellishment.[8] Puin states, "Such aberrations, although not surprising to textual historians, are troublingly at odds with the orthodox Muslims..."[9] Additionally, the Sana'a manuscripts were written in a form of Arabic that has no vowel markings or distinguishing marks, which means that an individual word can have up to thirty different meanings. Puin claims that "The sheer existence of so many different possible readings would suggest that this text wasn't passed down word for word. The text isn't as stable as it seems in the Cairo version."[10] There are also differences in the order of suras in the Sana'a manuscripts. Puin questions whether

---

[5] Ibid.

[6] Gerd Puin, as quoted in "The Oldest Qur'anic Manuscripts"
http://www.youtube.com/watch?v=iNdvsLh128Q (accessed August 9, 2011)

[7] Sujit Das. "Ancient Qur'anic Manuscripts of Sana'a and Divine Downfall" May 6, 2011

http://www.faithfreedom.org/articles/quran-koran/ancient-qur%e2%80%99anic-manuscripts-of-sana%e2%80%99a-and-divine-downfall/_(accessed August 9, 2011)

[8] Lester.

[9] Gerd Puin, as quoted in "Oldest Yemeni Quran differs from Uthman Quran today"

http://www.youtube.com/watch?v=OLSEaPxePZc&playnext=1&list=PLBBB589C38BF51
85E (accessed August 9, 2011).

[10] Ibid.

this means that most of the suras were not written down and put into approximately their final form during Muhammad's lifetime.[11]

Additionally, the Sana'a documents contain palimpsests, areas of parchment where the text was washed off and written over. Regarding the palimpsests, Dr. Patrick Sookhdeo states, "If the researchers are correct, particularly on dating, this suggests in fact that the Qur'an was not a single sought after, single entity that was fixed by 650 but actually developed much, much later; hence the overlaying of texts of written materials."[12]   Dr. Christoph Heger states,

> Why the older layer was wiped out cannot be said definitely until it can be read in detail.... Most probably the arrangement of the surahs was altered. And this hypothesis is corroborated by the fact that amongst the findings in Sanaa [sic] there are indeed Qur'ans with an *arrangement of surahs different* from the transmitted Qur'an.[13]

The discovery of the Sana'a documents, their dating, and their textual variations from today's Qur'an are of monumental significance in challenging the Muslim belief that the Qur'an is incorruptible, completely preserved in its current form.   Sujit Das states unequivocally that discovery of the Sana'a manuscripts:

> scattered the orthodox Muslim belief that the Qur'an as it has reached us today is quite simply 'the perfect, timeless, and unchanging Word of God.' It means the Qur'an has been distorted, perverted, revised, modified and corrected, and textual alterations had taken place over the years purely by Human hands....and the core belief of millions plus Muslims that the Qur'an is the eternal, unaltered word of God is now clearly visible as a great hoax, a totally downright falsehood.[14]

---

[11] Gerd Puin, "Observations on Early Qur'an Manuscripts in Sana'a" In *What the Koran Really Says: Language, Text and Commentary*, by Ibn Warraq. (Amherst, NY: Promethius Books, 2002), 742.

[12] Patrick Sookhdeo, as quoted in "The Oldest Qur'anic Manuscripts" http://www.youtube.com/watch?v=iNdvsLh128Q (accessed August 14, 2011)

[13] Christoph Heger, "A Qur'an Palimpsest from the Sanaa" Qur'ans http://www.christoph-heger.de/palimpse.htm (accessed August 14, 2011)

[14] Sujit Das, "Ancient Qur'anic Manuscripts of Sana'a and Divine Downfall"

http://www.faithfreedom.org/articles/quran-koran/ancient-qur%e2%80%99anic-manuscripts-of-sana%e2%80%99a-and-divine-downfall/ (accessed August 14, 2011)

Although not all would state it as polemically as Das, clearly the findings pose a challenge to the Muslim belief about the Qur'an.

What is the Muslim response? Several months after Toby Lester's article, Dr. Muhammad Mohar Ali published a review.[15] His main refutation is that although Lester claims that the Sana'a documents have unconventional verse ordering and minor textual variants, not a single example of any of these were given.[16] He concludes that "Puin and Lester have simply attempted to make a mountain out of a mole [sic] on the basis of inadequate, inconclusive, unclear and unspecified evidence."[17] Most of Ali's article centers on challenging other orientalists whom Lester refers to in his article. Ali's refutation is not an adequate one: Lester's article was not meant to be a detailed article for manuscript scholars, but one addressed to the lay public.

One popular Muslim website refutes the dating of the Sana'a manuscripts.[18] The author points out that although von Bothmer dated Codex Sana'a DAM 20-33 to around 710 – 715 AD, this date was vehemently argued by Jonathan Bloom. He quotes Bloom as saying, "there is no scientific proof for von Bothmer's claim that the manuscript has been carbon dated to the Umayyad period, and a ninth-century date seems more likely on the basis of script."[19] Furthermore, the author states that the resemblance of some codices to the "Great Umayyad Qur'an" suggests that the "Great Umayyad Qur'an" may have served as a model.[20] Regarding differences in the order of the suras in the Sana'a manuscripts, the author states "Simple logic dictates that if a person or patron wished to copy or have copied a few or even many *surahs* for personal or

---

[15] Muhammad Mohar Ali, *The Qur'an and the Latest Orientalist Assumptions: Being a Review of Toby Lester's Article: "What is the Koran?"* (Ipswich,UK: Jam'iat Ihyaa' Minhaaj Al-Sunnah, 1999).

[16] Ibid, 8-9.

[17] Ibid, 10.

[18] "The Qur'anic Manuscripts" http://www.islamic-awareness.org/Quran/Text/Mss/ (accessed August 14,2011).

[19] JM Bloom in "The Introduction Of Paper To The Islamic Lands And The Development Of The Illustrated Manuscript", *Muqarnas*, 2000, Volume XVII, pp. 22-23 (footnote 15) as quoted in

http://www.islamic-awareness.org/Quran/Text/Mss/yem1f.html (accessed August 14, 2011)

[20] "Codex Sana'a DAM 01-29.2 – A Qur'anic Manuscript From 2nd Century Of Hijra"

http://www.islamic-awareness.org/Quran/Text/Mss/yem2a.html (accessed August 14, 2011) public edification, he or they were not limited to copying *surahs* adjoining each other only."[21] The website provides a very academic and informative evaluation of some of the Sana'a manuscripts. It challenges some of the dates provided by von Bothmer and some of the sura ordering, but does not completely address the differences in text.

Muhammad Mustafa Al-A'zami also addresses Toby Lester's article on the Sana'a documents and claims that Lester's approach is purely academic, that of a "curious reporter filing an objective report," with no credentials to write on Islam except that he lived in Yemen and Palestine.[22] He compares Gerd Puin to a bookbinder who completes a magnificent binding of a mathematical text and therefore thinks he is a world authority on mathematics.[23] He claims that Puin has since denied most of the findings Lester ascribed to him.[24] Shortly after the publication of Lester's article in *The Atlantic*, Puin did indeed write a letter to al-Qadi Isma'il al-Akwah which was published in the Yemeni newspaper *ath-Thawra*. Al-A'zami translates part of Puin's letter as follows:

> The important thing, thank God, is that these Yemeni Qur'anic fragments do not differ from those found in museums and libraries elsewhere, with the exception of details that do not touch the Qur'an itself, but are rather differences in the way words are spelled. This phenomenon is well-known...[25]

Al-A'zami states that "This deflates the entire controversy, dusting away the webs of intrigue that were spun around Puin's discoveries and making them a topic unworthy of further speculation."[26] It seems that Puin's letter was more an effort in diplomacy, however, rather than a retraction of his assertions. Al-A'zami states: "There will never be a discovery of a Qur'an, fragmented or whole, which differs from the consensus text circulating throughout the world. If

---

[21] "Codex Sana'a DAM 01-27.1 – A Qur□nic Manuscript From Mid-1st Century Of Hijra" http://www.islamic-awareness.org/Quran/Text/Mss/soth.html (accessed August 14, 2011).

[22] Muhammad Mustafa Al-A'zami, *The History of the Qur'anic Text From Revelation to Compilation: A Comparative Study with the Old and New Testaments* (Leicester, England: UK Islamic Academy, 2003), 4.

[23] Ibid., 4.

[24] Ibid., 11.

[25] Ibid., 12.

[26] Ibid.

it does differ then it cannot be regarded as Qur'an, because one of the foremost conditions for accepting anything as such is that it conform [sic] to the text used in Uthman's Mushaf."[27] The Muslim belief about the Qur'an precludes the option to even question it. Al-A'zami doesn't adequately address the challenge posed by the Sana'a manuscripts; he simply disregards the issue.

Hamza Andreas Tzortzis has also written an article addressing the claims of Puin that there are discrepancies in the Sana'a manuscripts.[28] Tzortzis states that the claims of Puin are "clearly far-fetched and totally untenable."[29] Regarding the claim that there are some differences in the numbering of 'ayahs in some suras, Tzortzis states, "Such difference in the numbering of 'ayahs is acknowledged even by some classical Muslim scholars and it does not affect the text at all."[30] Regarding the palimpsests, Tzortzis states that palimpsests "do not suggest anything more than correction of mistakes omitted in the writing of the words in the first instance. It cannot be a proof in support of the theory of revision of evolution of the text unless an earlier copy of the Qur'an containing different words and expressions in the same place is shown to exist. This has not been found in the Sana'a manuscripts."[31] Tzortzis also states:

> the conclusion that the surahs were not written down in their final form during the lifetime of the Prophet or that a Qur'an with a different ordering of the surahs was in circulation for a long time just because two or three sheets have been found where some surahs have been written in a different order, that is surahs from different places of the Qur'an in circulation have been put together, is hasty and untenable....[32]

Interestingly, Tzortzis points out that Puin claims in a number of the Sana'a manuscripts the letter alif is written in a different way,

---

[27] Ibid., 13.

[28] Hamza Andreas Tzortzis, "Dr. Puin and the 'Yemeni' Manuscripts: Taken from 'The Qur'an & The Orientalists' by Mohar Ali"

http://hamzatzortzis.blogspot.com/2008/07/dr-puin-yemeni-manuscripts.html

(accessed August 14, 2011)

[29] Ibid.

[30] Ibid.

[31] Ibid.

[32] Ibid.

but doesn't address this issue. He concludes his article by saying that "The existence of a Qur'an with a different arrangement of the surahs or with what is called "corrections" and "revisions" cannot be cited as proof that such a Qur'an has ever been in use among the Muslims."[33] Once again, the issues are not totally addressed, but discarded as not possible.

The findings of the Sana'a manuscripts certainly present a challenge to the Muslim belief that the Qur'an of today is the perfect record of what was revealed to Muhammad. When confronted with the challenge of the Sana'a manuscripts most Muslims are not willing to address the specifics of textual criticism. The most academic discussion is found at www.islamic-awareness.org , and even this website does not address the discrepancies of the Sana'a manuscripts but only challenges the dating. To the Muslim, if an old manuscript is discovered that is different from the Qur'an of today, then by definition, this manuscript is not valid. The point is well said by F.E. Peters:

> When old Biblical manuscripts, parchments or ancient Hindu manuscripts are discovered, Christian and Hindu scholars almost climb over each other's shoulder to gain an early access to them. Such findings cause great excitement to them. But sadly, no such excitement exists in Islam. Christians and Hindus are eager to see more and more light shed on the earliest manuscripts of their scriptures, while Muslims resist, often with strong determination.[34]

Once evaluation of the Sana'a documents is completed, it likely will provide further challenge to the Muslim view that the Qu'ran has been maintained perfectly since the revelation to Muhammad, but Muslims will struggle to even consider this a possibility.

---

[33] Ibid.

[34] As quoted by Sujit Das. "Ancient Qur'anic Manuscripts of Sana'a and Divine Downfall"
http://www.faithfreedom.org/articles/quran-koran/ancient-qur%E2%80%99anic-manuscripts-of-sana%E2%80%99a-and-divine-downfall/ (accessed August 14, 2011).

The Bible, the Qur'an, and the space in between: Telling the Story

Brent Neely

Nazareth Evangelical Theological Seminary
Israel

What do we expect from a divinely-inspired book? To qualify as "revelation" must it answer all our questions? Must its language itself be somehow miraculous, almost super-human? Should it unveil the mysteries of modern science or be replete with uncannily accurate predictions? Must it inspire reverence from more people than any other book does? Who is to adjudicate these things?

In the contrast between the claims of Christian and Muslim faith there is probably no more fundamental arena of conflict than that of the "scriptures." In some sense *all* contested issues (from the Trinity to the crucifixion to the political nature of religion) lead back to the texts that are marshalled to support one's contentions. In the encounter between Christian and Muslim books, the polemical comparison between Bible and Qur'an is at times reduced to a contest over whose book is "best," truly "inerrant," or bears the surest marks of "inspiration."

Comparing Bible and Qur'an: The questions to ask

The "battle of the books" can easily become a frustrating exchange. Is *brass-knuckle* debate over the accuracy or flaws of either book the only option for us as believers? Might there be another angle for comparing the Christian and Muslim scriptures with their related but largely incommensurable messages?

The misdirection of much debate is partly due to the failure to consider prior questions like: *What is divine inspiration and what would it look like in a book anyhow? What about genre issues? What is the structure of faith; the character and purpose of God; the predicament of humanity; the nature of salvation?* Having very different views of God, humanity, and history, the two religions naturally have rather different expectations when it comes to the shape of en-scriptured revelation. There is, of course, an element of circularity to all this:

our expectations are shaped by the books we already accept as inspired. Nonetheless, I want to argue for the value of approaches to the comparison of Bible and Qur'an that focus elsewhere than on questions of accuracy/error, miracles of language, and so on. In the rest of the essay we will hone in on the contrasting notions of Salvation History evidenced in the Bible and the Qur'an.

Bible and Qur'an: Their retrospective views

An examination of the salvation-historical perspectives of these books involves some sense of the books' relation to prior "books," perhaps that of the Qur'an to the Bible (or *tawrat, injil,* etc.) or that of the New Testament to the Old Testament (Hebrew Bible). We must note in passing that the Qur'an alleges some sort of distortion or corruption (*tahrif*) of the former Scriptures. However, for present purposes, it is crucial to understand that here we are examining the Qur'an's own *idealized view* of the history of revelation; we are interested in its own conception of its relation to, say, the supposed "original" Torah or Gospel. Dealing with the charge that the current Bible has been "corrupted" is for another occasion.

The Christian Story

A critical problem in relating Muslim scripture to the Bible is precisely this matter of the glaringly different conceptions of salvation history. There is a major divide between what the Christian and Muslim books tell us that God has always been up to in our world. The biblical pattern might be outlined thusly: Creation → Fall → Covenant/Election → Exodus → Kingdom → Exile → Messianic Promise → Messianic Redemption → Final Conflict/Judgment → New Creation. The Biblical sweep can be refracted through different prisms, such as God's sovereign reign, the unfolding of divine glory, the story of redemption, and so on. The principal point is that on a Christian view, the Bible is a story, a God-centered drama of the universe in which humanity participates and experiences both his judgment and salvation.

For the Christian the Bible is a single, over-arching story with a beginning, middle, and end. God's promise to restore a radically sin-marred humanity is channelled through a man and nation (Abraham/Israel), but the chosen people too stand under judgment and in need of redemption. The story comes to a climax in an "end-time" intervention. According to prophetic promise, God himself acts in sacrificial love. God is unveiled in the shocking reversal of the death and resurrection of the messianic Son, Jesus of Nazareth. This establishes the restoration of the "overt" reign of God on his earth, the unseating of evil, the redemption of sinners, the start of a new creation—all to be confirmed and completed at the Second Coming.

For our purposes, three points about the Bible story need underlining:

1. The Grand Narrative of the Bible is progressive and developmental. Each stage strains forward to the next and is self-consciously incomplete, awaiting the looming climax. The stages of the story are not interchangeable and random in sequence. Abraham had to be called out, Israel had to emerge and be ransomed, Israel had to stumble in her vocation, etc., *and all in that order*. This necessary sequencing and a promise-fulfilment relationship is vital to the link between the Old and New Testaments, which have been likened to a seed (OT) which comes to full flower (NT).

2. The eschatological fulfilment represented by Jesus is the climactic, long-promised, yet surprising, fulfilment of ancient designs—designs built in to the beginning of the story. The Messiah comes as the realization of a prophetic promise. The new heavens and new earth are a resplendent, unprecedented reality, but they are still in continuity with what came before. The New Jerusalem of *Revelation* answers to the Eden of *Genesis*. God's good purposes for a world gone awry in the beginning are finally realized. A typological fulfilment pattern is a dominant hermeneutic in the New Testament's use of the Old.

3. In accomplishing the redemption and restoration of his world, Jesus comes in a long line of preceding leaders, messengers, and prophets, but he is far more than any of these. As "Son" and "Immanuel" he is not simply "the best in category"; he is alone in his category.

The Muslim Story

In one sense, it is not possible to discuss the Qur'anic view of (holy) history without reference to the Bible because of the conscious, direct, or allusive reference in the Qur'an to the prior revelations and prophets. At least nominally, a large number of "biblical" characters are taken as divinely-sent messengers. Examples include Adam, Noah, Abraham, Joseph, Moses, David, Jonah, Jesus, and others. Now, the Bible clearly is not a simple tale, written by a single author at one sitting; it must be read carefully across time and genres as a meta-story. Having said that, the Qur'an's structure is even less a seamless narrative by comparison. It is neither chronological nor principally designed as a story. However, one *can* detect an implied structure of reality behind its exhortations, commands, and allusive tales. There is an *implied* story, a salvation history.

The gist is that, from the start, the only overwhelmingly sovereign Creator-God calls all humanity to submission, obedience, and recognition of his unvarying oneness. From the failing of Adam and Eve onwards, humanity's problem has been one of straying, weakness, and temptation towards idolatry—our deficiency being a failure to take "guidance," our need for divine law. Humankind is prone to thanklessness and forgetfulness towards God. So, God repeatedly, throughout history, sends revelation as a "reminder" (e.g., Q 6 .68-72; 10.71). Humanity's "salvation" does not consist in a restoration from radical sinfulness to intimacy with a personal God—his essence remains inscrutable in any case. It lies rather with submission to his revealed will and with a turning from all idolatry, all "association" of anything else with him.

According to the Qur'an, through the long trail of history, God's dealings with recalcitrant humanity have entailed warnings, punishments, and beckoning back to the "straight path" through a series of prophets, "biblical" and otherwise. God's gracious guidance orders humanity's relationship to God and minutely structures society. The divine summons is proclaimed in the Qur'an against a backdrop of the approaching final judgment. At the last cataclysm, all will be raised from death to horrific torment in the Fire or limitless pleasures in Paradise. So, between creation and judgment we have an impressive succession of messengers culminating in the dispensation of Muhammad, the greatest, the final prophet. His scope is universal, and he is also "eschatological," at least in the sense that he brings the *final* (imminent?) warning of the coming Day. No new prophet is to emerge after him.

Thus, the Islamic appeal, which is sometimes detailed as a call to believe in God, the prophets, "the books," angels, the last day, and so on (Q 2.285; 4.136), may be boiled down to the charge to believe in "God and his messenger." The Messenger comes with a dire alert! The Day of Judgment thunders in the pages of the book, and each one awaits an awesome accounting based on some combination of works and the inscrutable will of God. For the blessed, the reward of Paradise awaits, for the damned, the Fire. The Qur'anic story may be one of prediction, promise and warning, reward and punishment, but it is not a biblical-style narrative pregnant with the themes of fulfilment and redemption.

Along with the Qur'anic conception of the human predicament and divine prescription comes a particular conception of the mission, role, and sequence of the former prophets and prior "books." In general the Qur'anic references to the prior scriptures understand the revelation given to Muhammad as one of confirmation of that which God sent before. So, even the mission of Jesus was quite like that of Muhammad himself. Jesus brought the Gospel[1] as guidance (*huda*), light (*nur*), and confirmation (*musaddiq*) of the Torah before him (cf. Q 5.46). The Qur'an may present Muhammad as the last prophet, but his dispensation is primarily a reiteration and renewal of God's guidance (e.g. Q 2.136; 3.3,48; 4.152; 9.111). Q 4.163: "We inspired you *as we inspired Noah and the prophets* after." Essentially, the various revelations are the same (Q 4.136). The relation of the Qur'an to the past is basically one of confirmation, repetition, and then supersession.

The Qur'an's use of the biblical base is terse and moralistic, apologetic, and provides a template for the prophet Muhammad himself. The former messengers predicted his coming; brought the same message; faced the same opposition and vindication; and fit the pattern of Muhammad's own ministry. If the Qur'an and the Bible were conjoined organisms to be surgically separated, a clean division could be achieved with relative ease. If, on the other hand, we had the same goal of separating the Old and New Testaments, the operation would be far more hazardous and intricate. We might say the two share a comprehensive vascular system. The Qur'an's depiction of its religious role is one of purification and restoration, sequentially final, but not linked to former revelation in

---

[1] Jesus is conceived of as a prophet bearing a revelation or a "book," the Gospel/*injil*.

such a way that a continued appropriation of it is dynamically essential.[2]

It may be the case that salvation history climaxes with the prophet and the "criterion" of his book (cf. Q 3.4), but it is hard to see his era as an *entirely new thing of a wholly different order*. There is no transposition to an altogether different key when we move from prior monotheisms to Islam as there is, for example, when we move from the dispensation of Moses to that of Jesus in the Gospel of John or the book of Hebrews. Though there are verses in the Qur'an assuming the prediction of Muhammad's mission in the former books (Q 61.6; 7.157; 48.29), there is no extended engagement of biblical texts showing how the trials and aspirations of God's people have been resolved with the sending of the Qur'an and its messenger. We have no typological fulfilment of the scriptures "in these last days," a realization, as the hymn would have it, of "the hopes and fears of all the years."

Certainly, for the Muslim, the prophet brought a life-example and revelation like no other, banishing the age of "ignorance" (*jahiliya*). Nonetheless, he at most represents the paradigm of "prophet" taken to the ultimate degree. Muhammad may be the "best and the last" in a succession of divine restorations, but, still, he does not represent a fundamentally distinct type of intervention by God on the order of Jesus the Son.

And what of the prophetic traditions (*hadiths*) which so often interpret the Qur'an for the Muslim? A famous tradition holds that all the "prophets are brothers." Muhammad comes in as something of a first among equals.[3] Very interesting is the comparison between Muhammad and Moses in the famous tradition in which, *at the resurrection, it will be unclear whether Muhammad or Moses first regains consciousness from the "cosmic swoon" before the rest of creation* (Bukhari 9.83.52).[4] Other *hadiths* tell us that Muhammad received six privileges unique to him among the prophets[5] or that he is like the final brick completing a splendid house (symbolizing the entirety of the prophets) [Bukhari 4.56.734]. The versions of the

---

[2] See J.D. McAuliffe's article in J. C. Reeves (ed.), *Bible and Qur'an: Essays in Scriptural Intertextuality*, Society of Biblical Literature, 2003, 108-110.

[3] Later popular and mystical legends super-exalting Muhammad are another matter.

[4] *Sahih Bukhari*, online at http://www.cmje.org/religious-texts/hadith/bukhari/ (accessed 5 September 2012).

[5] See, for example, standard commentaries on Q 33.40.

story of Muhammad's Ascent to Heaven likewise see the prophets as quite interchangeable, only with Muhammad coming in emphatically as the final one. The point is that even when the texts magnify the person of Muhammad over other prophets, we are still dealing with a difference of degree, not of kind.

Setting the two "revelations" side by side once again, the point is often made, but worth restating: In Islam, God's highest revelation to humanity is a book. In the Christian faith, it is a person, the Word made flesh. Both our books purport to bring "Good News," but their essences are in striking contrast. At its core, the Qur'an is an announcement (of promise and threat) from God, a command or "law," if you will. At its heart the Bible is a story of what a loving God has done for us in Christ.

Tell the story[6]

When it comes to witness across the religious and cultural divide, what might be the practical implications *related to the Christian-Muslim disjunction we have been describing*? Speaking from within the Christian fold, one option might be to look for ways to adapt or contextualize any presentation of our faith in line with Muslim expectation. However, the disjunction in salvation-historical schemes is hardly a peripheral or cosmetic matter. We are dealing with the very shape of reality and the metanarrative of what God is about in the world. Adjust too much and it is no longer the Christian faith that is being communicated!

Another possible response to the dilemma of the contrasting scriptures is one we have already mentioned. That is, of course, the intense apologetic effort to demonstrate the factual truth and miraculous nature of the Bible over against the Qur'an. This kind of endeavour is fraught with challenges and can elicit unintended consequences, but a few hardy debaters may well thrive in this fray.

I want to forward another suggestion which is neither "accommodationist" nor combatively polemical. Put very simply, "tell the story." As has been intimated, the Qur'an is a message, a summons, an eschatological warning, etc. But, for the most part, it is not a story. Narratives do appear in its pages, of course, but mainly in sequences alluding to the prophets. These allusive references throughout the text point to the *implied* "story" of Islamic

---

[6] I am thankful here for my access to an unpublished essay by Scott Bridger on *The Christian Use of the Qur'an.*

salvation history discussed above. The Christian Bible, on the other hand, not only is full of stories, but is best read as an entire story-- the record of God's action in his world. It is, in fact, *the* story, His Story. So for reasons spiritual, dogmatic, and structural it is no wonder that the biblical climax, the story of Christ crucified (and risen), is not what a Muslim is programmed to expect in the "*injil.*" But, we can also say, with great wonder and thanks, many Muslims *do* find that this story, this "foolishness," becomes for them the power and wisdom and redemption of God (1 Cor. 1)!

The Bible is the story around which our lives, all lives, Muslim lives, are meant to be oriented. It is the story of human need, divine grace, and the drama of salvation. It is the story we so need— God's own glorious, cosmic story. And the wonder of redemption is that the Lord invites us to join him in it. The Christian hope and plea is not so much to win a battle with the Muslim over the quality of one's book; it is that many from all backgrounds might encounter Christ in the pages of the Bible and find that with him are "the words of life." May the Spirit empower the telling of the story so that many may see the light of God's own glory shining in the face of Jesus (2 Cor. 4.6).

Christian Muslim Relations in Malaysia

Rev Dennis Raj

PhD Candidate
London School of Theology

Since the time of independence from the British in 1957, multi racial and multi religious Malaysia has generally enjoyed peaceful co-existence among its citizens. Only the racial riots of May 1969 stand out as a contrast to an otherwise largely harmonious journey. Yet some undercurrents have newly emerged that could potentially challenge the existing accord. One area of difficulty that has widened the gap between Christians and Muslims is the portrayal of Christianity as a threat to the primacy of Islam in Malaysia. Together with the issue of religion, political overtones are also added to make Christianity appear as a threat. These portrayals are the product of some politically motivated Malays and other Muslim quarters who view Christianity as a challenge to the overall Islamization agenda of the government.

Perceived threats of Christian proselytization

The issue of the alleged proselytization of Malays by Christians continues to be presented to Muslims as an impending danger for Muslims. In March 2012, the Johor State Education Department organized a seminar that was titled in Malay as: "*Pemantapan Aqidah, Bahaya Liberalisme dan Pluralism Serta Ancaman Kristianisasi Terhadap Umat Islam. Apa Peranan Guru?*" (Strengthening the Faith, the Dangers of Liberalism and Pluralism and the Threat of Christianity towards Muslims. What is the Role of Teachers?). Two religious teachers from each of the 55 national schools across the state of Johor were required to attend the compulsory seminar. The programme was jointly organized by JAKIM (Department of Islamic Authority Malaysia) with the help of the Johor Mufti Department and the Johor State Education Department. Asked to comment on the reality of a Christian threat that warrants such a seminar, the Johor Education Department Director stated: "... there is a threat to convert Muslims to Christians ... if someone is Muslim, he will be Muslim until he dies".[1]

The issue then generated different types of responses from different quarters. The Christian umbrella grouping CFM (Christian Federation of Malaysia) issued a media statement rejecting the portrayal of Christianity as a threat to other religions. Calling the threat as 'unfounded' and labeling the seminar as 'provocative', it reminded the government that this would not augur well for its efforts to showcase itself as a moderate Islamic nation.[2] CFM also added that the timing of the program could not have been worse as it was just weeks before, in February 2011, that the Deputy Prime Minister who is also the Minister of Education, Muhyiddin Yassin, launched an annual programme to promote inter-faith understanding in the schools. The non-Muslim religious minority grouping of MCCBCHST also released a press statement and expressed that such a seminar would threaten and undermine the already delicate religious harmony in Malaysia. [3] It even asked the Prime Minister to 'walk the talk' in his Islamic moderation views and his 'One Malaysia' slogan.[4] The 'One Malaysia' slogan was started by Prime Minister Najib after the ruling party lost its traditional two thirds majority in the Parliament during the March 2008 elections. It was promoted by the government as a feel-good factor to make all Malaysians feel included and not sidelined in any way.

In a news article, one Christian priest questioned the rationale for the seminar by asking how the threat could be possible in schools since all the curriculum was actually supplied and monitored by the Education Ministry officials themselves. He also added that even in the Christian mission schools, the government is in charge of appointing teachers and all the teachers are no longer allowed to

---

[1] 'Christian threat' seminar to strengthen Islamic faith, says Johor education authority, Lisa J Ariffin, 29th March 2012, <http://www.themalaysianinsider.com/malaysia/article/christian-threat-seminar-to-strengthen-islamic-faith-says-johor-education-authority/>

[2] "CFM Strongly Protests Provocative Seminar on Unfounded Christian threat to Muslims", CFM Media Statement, 30th March 2012

[3] Seminar will undermine religious harmony, Stephanie Santa Maria, 29th March 2012, <http://www.freemalaysiatoday.com/category/nation/2012/03/29/mccbst-seminar-will-undermine-religious-harmony/>

[4] Mr. Prime Minister Sir: time to walk your talk, MCCBCHST Press Statement 30th March 2011.

teach any non-Muslim religious classes or even hold prayer sessions.[5]

Some Muslim organizations, like the members of PEMBELA (Muslim Organisations in Defence of Islam), felt that it was well within the rights of Muslims to organize the event and said that opposition towards the event meant questioning the guaranteed rights of the Muslims.[6] PERKASA, a Malay rights group also defended the seminar and felt that the program needed to continue to defend against 'organised efforts to convert Muslims.'[7] When an official (who declined to be named) was asked if he had proof of proselytising by Christians, he answered that: "Even if there is no threat, we must be careful so that the faith of Muslims will not be influenced".[8] The Islamic Affairs Minister at the federal level also expressed that no quarters should feel wronged about the title as it was well within Muslims' rights to defend their own faith.[9] The *Persatuan Ulama Malaysia* (Malaysian Ulama Association) also felt that the Johor government should not be apologetic for organising the seminar as it is an Islamic administration and has a duty to do so. The matter was then brought up at the cabinet level, which decided that the wording of 'Christian threat' should be removed from the title of the seminar. One government minister then asked all parties to stop discussing the issue as the matter was now considered to be settled. Despite the stipulated change in the title, the Johor state Mufti assured that although the title may have been changed, the 'contents and structure' will remain unaltered in any way.[10] This was a clear indication that despite the misgivings from different quarters, some Muslims continue to feel that the Christian proselytization threat was a real and present danger for all Muslims in Malaysia.

---

[5] Seminar will undermine religious harmony, *Ibid.*

[6] PEMBELA says 'Christian Threat' seminar a 'guaranteed' Muslim right, By Shazwan Mustafa Kamal, 29th March 2012, <http://www.themalaysianinsider.com/malaysia/article/pembela-says-christian-threat-seminar-a-guaranteed-muslim-right/>

[7] PERKASA: 'Christian threat' seminars a must, Mohammad Farwan Darwis, 28th March 2012.

[8] PEMBELA says 'Christian Threat' seminar a 'guaranteed' Muslim right, *Ibid.*

[9] Minister defends 'Christian Threat' Seminar, Syed Jaymal Zahid, 29th March 2012, <http://www.freemalaysiatoday.com/category/nation/2012/03/29/minister-defends-christian-threat-seminar/>

[10] Tsu Koon says 'Christian Threat' seminar is state government's prerogative, Shannon Teoh, 5th April 2012, < http://www.themalaysianinsider.com/malaysia/article/tsu-koon-says-christian-threat-seminar-is-state-governments-prerogative/>

Threats from Indonesia

Some influential Muslim quarters have also argued that the existence of Indonesia with its large population of Christians is a potential threat for Muslims in Malaysia. Writing on the subject, one member of the Panel of Islamic Consultative Council and *Wasatiyyah* in the Prime Minister's Department, Ridhuan Tee Abdullah, alleged that rapid Christianization was taking place in Indonesia. He said that although Indonesia is currently the largest Muslim country in the world, the rapid spread of Christianity would mean that Indonesia could lose its Muslim majority status in the near future. In an article in *Sinar Harian*, a popular Malay language newspaper, he presented statistics that showed that although Indonesia used to be 90 per cent Muslim, it was now recording only 200 million Muslims out of a total population of 240 million.[11] His speculative article appeared in his own weekly column called '*Buka Minda*' (Open Your Mind) in the said newspaper. As a national council member of PERKIM (The Muslim Welfare Organization of Malaysia) and as Associate Professor in the National Defence University, his views are taken seriously by the Muslim fraternity in Malaysia. In the related article, Tee who is an ethnic Chinese and a convert to Islam, cited a passage from *Surah Al-Anfal* in the Qur'an and appeared to suggest that because of their proselytization efforts, Christians could also be construed as the 'enemy' of Muslims. He mentioned that Christians had great financial power around the world and the Malay Archipelago had now become their main target for proselytization efforts. He warned that in future, the Christians and their evangelical movements could attempt to employ similar tactics in Malaysia as well. He ended the article by calling on Muslims in Malaysia to 'save' their fellow Muslim brethren in the Indonesian archipelago.

The Malaysian government's ban on the Alkitab, the Indonesian Bible is also directly related to the fear of Indonesian Christian influence. These threats were being directly construed from some of the conversion cases that had happened in Indonesian soil. The Government feels that allowing a free flow of Malay language Bibles and other Christian material from Indonesia would encourage Christians to use them for the purpose of converting the Malays. These conversions are then interpreted by the government

---

[11] *Selamatkan Aqidah Umat Islam* (Save the Faith of the Muslims), Ridhuan Tee Abdullah, 6th August 2010, <http://www.sinarharian.com.my/kolumnis/ridhuan-tee-abdullah/selamatkan-akidah-umat-islam-1.73955>

as a ploy of the Christians to weaken the Malay race's power base in the country, as the constitution does not regard a Malay person as belonging to the Malay race unless he remains a Muslim. Writing about the suspected danger of using Islamic words to proselytize Muslims, a prominent Islamic law scholar in Malaysia, Mohammad Hashim Kamali wrote:

> "Christians in Indonesia had reportedly imitated some of the Muslim traditional practices and expressions in an effort to entice Muslims to participate in their activities." [12]

Conclusion

Although on the one hand the Malaysian government has been championing the use of Malay language as the national language, a sense of suspicion and fear of Christians' true motives seems to override the need to allow for an open flow and usage of the language.

This fear is compounded when Muslim political leaders sensationalize religious issues for their own political advantage.

---

[12] Mohammad Hashim Kamali, *Islamic Law in Malaysia: Issues and developments* (Kuala Lumpur: Ilmiah Publishers, 2000) 185

Disputed Churches in Indonesia

Dr Peter Riddell

Vice Principal (Academic), MST

"Places of worship have become a topic of much dispute around the world in recent years", said Dr Melissa Crouch at the launch of a new report at the Melbourne University Law School on June 26. last. "Examples are the Swiss ban on minarets in 2009 and the 2010 Ground Zero mosque dispute in New York city," she added.

Her talk focused on a report entitled "Disputed Churches in Jakarta", published in Indonesian by the Center for Religious and Cross-Cultural Studies of Gadjah Mada University in Yogyakarta and translated into English by the Melbourne Law School.

Indonesia has witnessed a significant increase in attacks on churches since the fall of the Suharto regime in 1998. An average of fifteen such attacks occurred each year between 1968-98, but a staggering 232 churches were damaged or destroyed between 1999-2001 alone.

The new report is based on extensive fieldwork by Indonesian researchers from the Jakarta-based Paramadina Foundation's Research Team into controversies. It particularly considers disputes relating to the construction of churches in Jakarta and the surrounding areas.

Between 1969-2006 the method of obtaining permits for new houses of worship was vague, said Dr Crouch. "The decision was largely left up to the village head. But under pressure of the increasing attacks on churches, in 2006 the Indonesian government introduced a new Joint Regulation 8 & 9."

This allowed for the creation of an Inter-Religious Harmony Forum, including representatives from Indonesia's six official religions. Dr Crouch explained further that "accompanying this new body was the 90/60 requirement, stipulating that 90 supporting signatures were needed from the community constructing the new house of worship, with a further 60 supporting signatures needed from other religious groups in the area."

The Report's findings

Interviews were held at fourteen different Catholic and Protestant church locations in Jakarta. The report identified the churches according to several categories.

First were churches experiencing no disputes over their establishment. Only one church fell into this category, a church located within an Indonesian Army settlement base.

The second category applied to churches that had resolved disputes. Six fell into this category, such as St Michael's Catholic Church, which had a membership of 10,000. Church leaders had obtained the necessary government permit but the community was subsequently put under pressure by the local Islamic community, with mosque sermons being very critical of the new church. The church leadership reached out to the Muslim community leaders, relationships flourished and the problem was resolved.

A further category relates to those churches encountering ongoing opposition to their construction. The GKI-Yasmin church in Bogor had been given approval to build that was subsequently cancelled by the local mayor. The church won on appeal but the mayor is still refusing to recognize the court decision and the valid permit. Local police complicity has resulted in a stalemate. Dr Crouch added that "it is important to note the support that the church has received from the local traditionalist Muslim group, the Nahdatul Ulama," in opposition to more militant Islamic opposition.

The report identified a fear of Christianisation as a key factor among Muslim communities opposing church construction. It also highlighted the complicit role of local bureaucracies, with many government officials bowing to pressure from Islamist militant groups such as the Islamic Defenders Front.

The report can be freely downloaded at http://www.law.unimelb.edu.au/melbourne-law-school/news-and-events/news-and-events-details/diaryid/6115

This article first appeared in "The Melbourne Anglican", August 2012, p5

The Future of Afghanistan

Dr Martin Parsons

Director of Faculty, Lowestoft Sixth Form College,
Suffolk, UK

Afghan history

Afghanistan is Persian for 'land of the Afghans', 'Afghan' being a local synonym for the Pushtun tribes. Whilst modern historians tend to date the history of modern Afghanistan from 1747 when the Pushtun tribes agreed to unite under the leadership of Ahmad Shah Abadali, this was hardly the creation of a modern state. More than a century later, the Amir Abdur Rahman Khan (1880-1901) conquered the non Pushtun areas of Afghanistan. These included the northern areas populated by groups including Tajiks and other Farsi (Persian) speakers, Uzbeks and Turkoman, the central areas populated by the Shi'a Hazaras and the Hindu Kush populated by animistic tribes that the Amir renamed Nuristanis ('people of the land of heavenly light') to commemorate his forcible conversion of them to Islam.

Prior to the 1979 Soviet invasion even university educated Afghans typically thought of themselves primarily in terms of their tribal identity as Pushtuns or Hazaras etc rather than as citizens of Afghanistan. For many Afghans it was only when they fled as refugees to countries such as Pakistan, where aid workers and other westerners referred to them as 'Afghans' that this became the way they began to think of themselves.

Following the Soviet withdrawal in 1989 the country became ruled by various *mujahiddin* warlords who controlled different regions of the country and fought each other for control of the central government. The main differences between these groups were not merely religious (Islamist or traditionalist and Sunni/Shi'a), but also ethnic with, for example, the Islamist Jamiyat-i-Islami led by Rabbani and Massoud being predominantly Tajik, while the Hezb-i-Islami led by Hekmatyar being mainly Pushtun. Similarly, the Taliban – a movement that emerged among students in Deobandi madrassas (Islamic theological schools) in 1994 has always been

43

predominantly Pushtun. Consequently, whatever happens to Afghanistan following the withdrawal of western military forces in 2014 is likely to be significantly determined by the ethnic faultlines of the Pushtun/non Pushtun divide.

What has changed post 9/11?

In examining the likely outcomes for Afghanistan after 2014, it is worthwhile to reflect on the changes that the western intervention since 2001 has brought about. In addition to the removal of an international terrorist organisation that aimed to impose Islamic government and *sharia* on the entire world, two areas stand out – human rights and economic development.

Human rights

When the *mujahiddin* were in charge of various areas of Afghanistan, most of them imposed a form of radical Islam that was somewhat stricter and more brutal than many people's traditional religious observance, especially in the cities. Shopkeepers were beaten up with sticks and forced to go into the mosque to pray; there were some girl's schools operating, but life for women outside the home was extremely restrictive. The Taliban massively increased this, closing down girl's education, forbidding women to be on the streets without a male relative. This was despite there being thousands of war widows with no family who had no means of survival other than street begging. Religious minorities were persecuted, Afghans found to be Christians were executed, while Sikhs and Hindus were forced to wear yellow badges similar to those the Nazis forced on the Jews. One of the most positive aspects of the western military intervention has been the growth of freedom for women and minorities due in large measure to the remit of the International Security Assistance Force (ISAF) including the protection of minorities. This freedom has been welcomed by many of the more educated Afghans living in the cities, particularly Kabul. However, it is highly questionable how long it will last after 2014, particularly in the more outlying cities.

Economic development

One of the most positive aspects of the western intervention has been the growth of the economy. Prior to 2001 there were almost no factories at all in Afghanistan – just a few bombed out former ones. Although there was some small scale industry such as the lapis lazuli mines in Badakhshan, there was little international trade.

Unemployment was widespread, teachers in government schools were often paid only for two months of the year. Apart from money changers, taxi drivers and shop keepers, only employees of aid agencies had reasonable wages. Moreover there was almost no infrastructure, which in some ways reflected the fact that unlike Pakistan, Afghanistan had never been a European colony. There were roads between cities, but their use by Soviet tanks had left so little tarmac on them that it was generally easier to avoid the small islands of tarmac. The telephone system was almost non existent. Much of that has changed now. The flood of aid agencies arriving since 2001 has not only significantly improved basic health and education, but also boosted the economy, although the departure of westerners after 2014 is likely to reduce GDP significantly. However, US geologists have discovered some of the world's largest supplies of copper and iron as well what may prove to be the world's largest supply of lithium creating the opportunity for significant export growth. These create the potential for a tax base that could fund basic services such as health and education. Nonetheless, these are just economic opportunities; if fighting breaks out again Afghanistan's economy and infrastructure could quickly go back to where it was before 2001. Peace and law and order is an essential requirement for economic growth.

The future after 2014

There are a number of cultural, religious and historical factors that provide clues to the likely state of Afghanistan after the withdrawal of the main western military forces in 2014:

The waiting strategy - Pushtun culture

The Taliban are a predominantly Pushtun grouping. The Pushtun tribal code known as *Pushtunwali* places two hugely important cultural duties on every Pushtun man. First, giving hospitality (*Melmastia*) including providing sanctuary (*nanawati*) to anyone asking for it. This duty made western demand to hand over bin Laden after 9/11 almost impossible to accede to. Secondly, taking blood vengeance (*badal*) on the extended family of anyone who has killed a member of his own extended family. This does not necessarily happen immediately, but involves waiting until the most opportune time, even if that is twenty years later. As the Taliban are predominantly Pushtun it would be extraordinarily naïve to think that their current strategy does not involve similar waiting until after the preannounced western withdrawal date before they launch their main offensive.

The Pushtun/non Pushtun ethnic faultline

As the Afghan National Army (ANA) is 97% Farsi speaking, after 2014 it is likely to be strongest and most loyal in Farsi speaking areas particularly Kabul and to lesser degree the Northern areas such as Panjshir and Badakhshan. Conversely, the ANA will face its greatest challenges in the Pushtun areas of the south and east such as Uruzgan and Helmand provinces where the ANA is currently being mentored by Australian and British forces respectively.

The rural-urban divide

Whilst the ANA is likely to control Kabul and probably major cities, it is much less likely to retain control more than temporarily of outlying rural areas. Prior to the 2001 western intervention successive Afghan governments had at best minimal control of most of these areas, particularly those at some distance from Kabul. There is therefore likely to be a rural-urban divide as well as an ethnic one.

The waiting warlords

That does not automatically mean that the Taliban will take over either the rural or even the Pushtun areas. There are two other possibilities: first, local tribal control based on village elders (*maliks*) and councils (*shuras*) which is the traditional form of government in much of Afghanistan; secondly, the warlords who fought each other for control prior to 2001 still have considerable power because the Karzai government set up under western auspices after the 2001 intervention was a coalition government. These warlords lead groups that fought as *mujahiddin* (holy warriors) in the *jihad* (holy war) declared against the Soviet invaders. However, such *mujahiddin* commanders are not part of traditional Afghan culture. They were originally young men with guns who gained power at the expense of the old men, the grey beards, who are the traditional elders in Afghan society. They are also predominantly radical Islamists in contrast to the traditionalist Islam of wider Afghan society, which whilst fundamentalist by western standards was not overtly political. In the opinion of many ordinary Afghans the 'good people' got out of the *mujahiddin* when the Russians left. The remaining groups led by regional warlords had a reputation not just for butchery, but also for looting and rape. During this time there was significant ethnic and religious 'cleansing', with the Hazara ethnic group who are Shi'a being particularly targeted by a number of Sunni *mujahiddin* groups. A reoccurrence of this is a distinct possibility after 2014.

Two particular groups pose an immediate danger to the Afghan government after 2014, the Haqqani network and the Hezb-i-Isami group led by Gulbaddin Hekmatyar. The Haqqani movement which eventually emerged from a split in Hezb-i-Islami has engaged in a significant level of attacks on western forces. In contrast, Hezb-i-Islami appears to be playing a waiting game. Hekmatyar's ambition for power is chilling. Following the Soviet withdrawal, he was offered the position of prime minister in a coalition government of other *mujahiddin* groups, but despite reportedly being urged by Bin Laden to accept it, he instead shelled a large area of Kabul to destruction because he wanted to be president. Hekmatyar (b.1947) appears to be biding his time, allowing other groups to fight western and ANA forces while his Hezb-i-Islami forces conserve their energies to enter the contest for power after the withdrawal of western forces in 2014.

President Karzai

Central to the future of Afghanistan will be the election of a new president in 2014 as President Karzai's maximum two terms come to an end just as western forces are withdrawing. Hamid Karzai is a unique figure in Afghan politics, educated at Cambridge University, head of the royal (Popalzai) clan of the Pushtuns, he also has had significant credibility with Farsi speakers.

The longer term

Any return of the Taliban or other radical Islamist groups to control of part or all of Afghanistan would mean the brutal imposition of *sharia* in a similar manner to the way the Taliban enforced it before 2001. However, Afghan history shows that whenever there has been a clash between *Pushtunwali*, the Pushtun tribal code, and *sharia*, *Pustunwali* has always won with mullahs in fact being regarded as outsiders in Pushtun society. The classic example of this was the case of Sayyid Ahmad Shah Bareli who led a Taliban like movement in the early part of the nineteenth century. However, when he preached against Pushtun marriage customs, the Pushtun tribes conspired against him and murdered both him and his immediate followers one night in 1831. Pushtun ballads are still sung in memory of this event. It is this anti clericalism in Pushtun tribal culture that may ultimately cause a Taliban revival to burn out.

It would therefore appear that best long term strategy for western governments to adopt would be to aim initially at a return to conditions similar to those experienced in Afghanistan prior to the Soviet invasion. Then the outlying rural areas were largely under the control of tribal law, which whilst harsh by western standards is, unlike the *sharia* which the Taliban brutally enforced, not an expansionist ideology. However, in major cities, particularly Kabul and amongst the educated elite, such as senior civil servants and professors, there was increasing western and liberal influences which were slowly filtering out to wider society. In some respects they have quietly continued to do so, albeit somewhat more covertly, throughout the trauma of the last thirty three years. It is this long term strategy that the West must now engage in, if Afghanistan is not again to become a haven for radical Islamists intent on plotting terror attacks on the West as part of their strategy to force the West to accept Islamic government and *sharia*.

Church and Mosque in Sub-Saharan Africa

Dr Peter Riddell

When we think about Islam and Christianity in Africa, one's first thought is to identify Muslim majorities in the north of the continent and Christian majorities in the central and southern parts of Africa. Indeed, this is generally true; we could draw a line from west to east cutting through the centre of Nigeria, southern Chad, the southern part of Sudan and through central Ethiopia, turning down the east coast and following the coast to stop at the ocean in the south of Tanzania. Above the line is largely Islamic; below the line is largely Christian.

This was not always the case, however. As recently as 1900, Christians only represented 9 percent of the population living below the Sahara Desert, and Muslims only represented 14 percent. The vast majority of the Sub-Saharan African population at that time followed African traditional religions in some form or other. By way of contrast, today the latter group only constitutes 13 percent of Sub-Saharan Africans, having seen their numbers plummet through mission activities by Christians (now 57 percent) and Muslims (now 29 percent). The vast region of Sub-Saharan Africa now plays host to 1/5 of the world's Christians and 1/7 of the world's Muslims.[1]

Of course, the dividing line merely masks the fact that both Christians and Muslims can be found as minorities, where the other is in the majority. This fact creates the potential for rivalry and, at times, violent conflict. In the regions where Islam and Christianity are intermixed, relationships vary from co-existence to violent conflict, with some observers seeing the dividing areas as "a volatile religious fault-line".

Of course, not all violent conflicts in Sub-Saharan Africa are related to religion. We need only consider the killing of over one million people in the Rwandan conflict in 1994. The competing Tutsis and Hutus were closely related in terms of ethnicity, culture and religion. Moreover, in Nigeria, where there is Christian-Muslim conflict in the north, there are often violent conflicts in the South

---

[1] http://pewresearch.org/pubs/1564/islam-christianity-in-sub-saharan-africa-survey, accessed 6 August 2012

that do not bear on religion in any way. In the words of Laila Al-Marayati (who served on the U.S. Commission for Religious Freedom):

> "...instability and volatility [in Nigeria] is simmering right beneath the surface... Some would say it's because Muslims want to impose Islam on others. But others would say the cause is corruption, Nigerian politics, the problems with coming out of a dictatorial system and trying to manage a democracy. Talk to someone from Nigeria about tribal issues. In the southern part of Nigeria, Muslims and Christians get along fine. Often, it has to do with who has the most resources in any place. If one group feels the other one is doing better economically, it becomes a problem."[2]

It would be good at this point to take an insider view as much as is possible. What do Sub-Saharan Africans themselves have to say about interreligious matters? We are helped in this by a public opinion survey conducted in early 2009 by the Pew Forum, based on 25,000 interviews in 19 countries in Sub-Saharan Africa.[3] From these interviews, a portrait of the diversity of Sub-Saharan Africans, both Christians and Muslims, was drawn up.

The first and perhaps most striking conclusion was the extent of religiosity in the countries surveyed. Unlike Western countries, where the majority of people still identify themselves as Christian but rarely attend worship, in Sub-Saharan Africa, the vast majority of people are active in practicing their faith, whether Christianity, Islam or an African traditional religion.

Nevertheless, although adhering to Christianity or Islam, many Sub-Saharan Africans practice a form of their faith which still bears striking influences from African traditional religion. Witchcraft is widespread, sacrifices are made to ancestors and spirits, and traditional religious healers have a steady supply of clients.

In terms of how Christians and Muslims view each other across the countries surveyed, there is widespread ignorance regarding knowledge of the other faith. Nevertheless, the survey suggested that many Muslims make a positive assessment of Christians in

---

[2] Pat McCaughan, "Muslim-Christian Conflict: Two women look beneath the surface", http://www.thewitness.org/archive/march2003/muslimchristian.html, accessed 6 August 2012.

[3] http://pewresearch.org/pubs/1564/islam-christianity-in-sub-saharan-africa-survey, accessed 6 August 2012

terms of tolerance and honesty, while contrastingly over 40 percent of Christians surveyed in 12 of the nations considered Muslims to be violent. An obvious question to be asked here relates to the respective life histories of Jesus and Muhammad.

While the majority of people surveyed express support for democracy and religious freedom, there was equally solid support for government based on either the Bible or Sharia Law among Christians and Muslims respectively. Herein lie the ingredients for religious conflict, especially when large numbers of Muslims surveyed express support for Sharia punishments such as stoning.

The Sharia question appears to be a source of considerable debate among Muslims, with numbers roughly evenly divided between those who want to impose veiling upon women and those who do not. While on matters relating to women, some Muslim majority countries, especially Mali and Djibouti, widely practice circumcision of young girls, although, tragically, this practice is reportedly more common among Christians than Muslims in Uganda.

Eschatological expectancy seems to be commonplace among both Christians and Muslims in Sub-Saharan Africa. At least 50 percent of Christians surveyed across the region anticipated the return of Jesus in their lifetimes. Meanwhile, 1 in 3 Muslims surveyed anticipated the reestablishment of the Caliphate, the central authority of Sunni Islam, in their own lifetimes. Where violence between Christians and Muslims does occur, the potential for such violence quickly spreading beyond immediate combatants is explained by the fact that at least 20 percent of Sub-Saharan Africans interviewed for this survey considered violence against civilians to be acceptable if it was in defence of one's religion.

While there is much tension between Christians and Muslims in certain locations in Sub-Saharan Africa, and these tensions and conflicts are likely to grow in coming decades, the Pew Forum Survey does not suggest that either faith is significantly encroaching upon the other in terms of numbers of conversions between them. The Survey reports that "there is virtually no net change in either direction through religious switching." There is one exception to this however; namely Uganda. Of the Christians and Muslims interviewed in that country, 1/3 of the Christians were Muslim Background Believers. In contrast, few Ugandan Muslims interviewed had converted from Christianity.

In conclusion, while Christians and Muslims living near each other in Sub-Saharan Africa do not always end up in conflict, some Christian-Muslim conflicts do erupt and will continue to do so. In an environment where Arab petrol dollars are being used to fund mosque construction and Islamic community expansion, and with the rise of jihadi sentiment in certain locations, the Christian-Muslim relationship in Sub-Saharan Africa is more likely to worsen than to ease in coming years. Given the fact that 20 percent of the world's Christians are found in the Sub-Saharan region, it is incumbent on the Church in the rest of the world to watch the Sub-Saharan African situation closely and to respond appropriately when needed.

Mali and Nigeria: Islamism at the gate

Elizabeth Kendal

Adjunct Research Fellow
CSIOF, MST

In 1991, the Algerian government cancelled the 2nd round of elections when it became clear that the Islamic Salvation Front (an Islamists party) was set to win. The Islamists responded violently, dragging the country in a bloody civil war which raged until peace was brokered in 2002. Rejecting peace, the Salafist Group for Preaching and Combat (GSPC) retreated to the desert, maintaining ties and sympathies with al Qaeda.

In November 2002, the US launched its Pan Sahel Initiative (PSI) – a US State Department funded program to assist the governments of Mauritania, Mali, Niger and Chad with countering the movement of trans-national terrorists through the Sahel. The program was expanded in 2005 into the Trans-Sahara Counterterrorism Initiative, and then subsequently into Operation Enduring Freedom – trans-Sahara.

In September 2006 al-Qaeda deputy Ayman al-Zawahiri announced al-Qaeda's "blessed union" with the GSPC. In January 2007, to reflect the new reality, the GSPC changed its name to **al-Qaeda in the Islamic Maghreb (AQIM).**

By working in co-operation with North Africa's US-allied anti-Salafi dictators, US counterterrorism initiatives managed to keep AQIM effectively hamstrung. However, the Arab Spring changed everything: AQIM is no longer contained.

This provides the context for the massive escalation in Islamic jihad, terrorism and persecution we are witnessing in Northern Mali and Northern Nigeria.

MALI

Traditionally a nomadic Muslim people, the Tuareg dominated the trans-Saharan caravan routes for millennia, until the 20th century, when the imposition of borders, natural desertification, urbanisation and the rise of maritime trade totally disrupted the Tuareg way of life.

In their quest to survive, the Tuareg launched separatist rebellions against the governments of Mali and Niger in 1963, 1990-95 and 2007-09. They also migrated north in search of work, which many found with the Libyan dictator Muammar Gaddafi, either as mercenaries or as soldiers in his African Legion. And while legitimate, legal trans-Saharan trade may have dried up, the Tuareg found they could still put their unique expertise to work smuggling illicit goods through the Sahara for criminals and terrorists. [1]

During this time, the Malian government not only failed to address legitimate Tuareg grievance, they exacerbated and compounded grievance through brutal crackdowns and repeated betrayals. In the French and US-assisted peace deal of 2005, the Malian government promised to decentralise government and give the Tuareg a greater degree of autonomy. They promised to provide practical assistance and incorporate Tuareg fighters, who had been trained in counterterrorism by US Special Forces, into the Malian military. Had these promises been honoured, then Mali may well have evolved into a stronghold *against* al-Qaeda, rather than a failed and fractured state overrun with foreign terrorists.

THE ARAB SPRING

From mid 2011, as Gaddafi's regime slowly crumbled, some 800 cashed-up, well-armed and well-trained Tuareg fighters, knowing their salaries were coming to an end, simply packed up and returned to Mali taking with them weaponry, ammunitions and military vehicles stolen from Gaddafi's arsenals. Among the returning fighters was Ibrahim Ag Bahanga, the leader of the 2007 Tuareg separatist rebellion. Bahanga, who had fled to Libya when peace was brokered in 2009, re-emerged in northern Mali in August 2011 vowing to reignite the rebellion. He was assassinated, most probably by a US-trained Malian counterterrorism unit, within hours of issuing his threat by satellite phone.[2]

Ag Mohamed Najem, a former Libyan Army colonel, subsequently took charge, renewing the Tuareg rebellion under the banner of the National Movement for the Liberation of Azawad (MNLA).

---

[1] Stratfor Global Intelligence *The Tuaregs – from African nomads to smugglers and mercenaries*, 6 February 2012

[2] Stratfor Global Intelligence *Mali Besieged by Fighters Fleeing Libya*, 2 February 2012

This proved disastrous for the dispirited, under-paid, poorly equipped and over-stretched Malian military. In late January 2012, Tuareg militia overran the Malian army garrison at Aguelhok, in the far north; their success due largely to the fact that the Malian soldiers had insufficient ammunition. When mobile phone footage reached Bamako, of rebels summarily executing nearly a hundred captive Malian soldiers, tensions soared. What happened in Bamako on 22 March 2012 was firstly a spontaneous mutiny led by junior soldiers refusing deployment without proper supplies, followed by a military coup.[3] The move was condemned internationally as undemocratic.

The National Movement for the Liberation of Azawad (MNLA) moved quickly to exploit the chaos and insecurity in Bamako. By 30 March 2012 they had captured Kidal; by 31 March, Gao; and by 1 April, Timbuktu. It was a violent and bloody rebellion. All aid agencies were sacked and looted. Banks were robbed and hospitals were ransacked. Reports emerged of killings and pack-rapes.

On 5 April 2012, the MNLA declared Azawad (northern Mali) an independent state.

But the MNLA had not conquered the north alone; for allied to the MNLA was Ansar Dine, an **al-Qaeda in the Islamic Maghreb (AQIM)**-linked jihadist militia with an agenda of its own.

Presenting themselves as non-separatists and restorers of order, Ansar Dine moved quickly to arrest Tuareg excesses and win hearts and minds. Hoisting the black flag of al-Qaeda, they declared the imposition of Sharia law. But any hopes Malians had faded fast as it became apparent that well-armed foreign fighters willing to cut the throats of Tuareg looters were never going to be the friends of any largely-secularised Malian.

Churches were torched and at least one pastor, along with his whole family, was executed. Fearing for their lives, northern Mali's Christians fled. They are now displaced in the south and across the wider region. Food is in short supply.[4]

---

[3] Andrew McGregor *Hot Issue — Mayhem in Mali: Implications of the Military Coup in Bamako* 23 March 2012, The Jamestown Foundation (analyzing Eurasia)

http://www.jamestown.org/single/?no_cache=1&tx_ttnews[tt_news]=39177

[4] Elizabeth Kendal *MALI: Christians flee as jihadists seize control of north,*
11 April 2012 Religious Liberty Monitoring
http://elizabethkendal.blogspot.com.au/2012/04/mali-christians-flee-as-jihadists-seize.html

In late May 2012, the Islamists seized a massive, secret, underground weapons and ammunition depot belonging to the Malian Army in Gao. A regional security source confirmed the seizure, saying the vast cache of weapons will greatly boost al-Qaeda in the Islamic Maghreb's (AQIM's) striking power, adding that the group "is today more armed than the combined armies of Mali and Burkina Faso". A Mauritanian diplomat commented: "We are in an early stage of Afghanistan and Somalia. There is no doubt in my mind."[5]

The rebels have also seized three major airstrips in the north, near the towns of Gao, Timbuktu and Tessalit. In the absence of a functioning Malian air force, the Islamists can ferry in anything they want, including drugs, weapons and more foreign fighters.

On 26 May 2012, the Arabic-speaking leadership of the MNLA signed a protocol for power-sharing with the Islamists. On 28 May, the French-speaking leadership of the MNLA renounced it revealing a profound split between the Arabic-speaking Tuareg who had spent decades in Libya, and the French-speaking Tuareg who had remained in Mali.[6]

The fact that the Tuareg are profoundly divided made little difference to the reality on the ground: the Islamists were the strongest force and by late June they had routed the MNLA and declared themselves to be full control of northern Mali.[7]

Sharia is being aggressive enforced through beatings, stonings and amputations, despite courageous public protests against it.[8] Cultural heritage is being destroyed.[9]

No longer demanding an independent state, the MNLA, says it is ready to fight *against* the Islamists. In early November 2012 West African leaders at an emergency ECOWAS summit agreed on a

[5] Elizabeth Kendal *MALI: Islamist's weapons seizure will greatly boost AQIM's striking power*, 5 June 2012
http://elizabethkendal.blogspot.com.au/2012/06/mali-islamists-weapons-siezure-will.html
[6] ibid

[7] Elizabeth Kendal *Mali: Islamists oust Tuareg-nationalists MNLA – making the reality official*, 29 June 2012
http://elizabethkendal.blogspot.com.au/2012/06/mali-islamists-oust-tuareg-nationalist.html

[8] *Islamists conduct amputations in Mali*, AP, 10 Sept 2012
http://www.huffingtonpost.com/huff-wires/20120910/af-mali-amputations/

[9] Elizabeth Kendal *Mali: Islamists destroy heritage and take human shields*, 4 July 2012
http://elizabethkendal.blogspot.com.au/2012/07/mali-islamists-destroy-heritage-and.html

3,300-strong force to wrest control of northern Mali from Islamist fighters.[10] The Mauritanian diplomat's nightmare scenario of a new "Afghanistan and Somalia" looms large.

NIGERIA

While the situation in Nigeria is different to that in Mali, there are many striking similarities.

Traditionally a nomadic Muslim people, the Fulani, like the Tuareg, have been negatively affected by 20th century trends. For centuries the Fulani grazed and watered their cattle along traditional routes until desertification -- caused mostly by deforestation, as wood is burned as fuel -- forced them to migrate south in search of grazing land, water and jobs. Where the Muslim "settlers" meet the predominantly Christian "indigenes", competition for land, water, jobs and political domination can be fierce.

While the Malian government spent decades *failing* to address legitimate Tuareg grievance, in Nigeria, successive Northern Muslim military dictators spent decades *empowering* the Fulani.

In 1991, President (General) Ibrahim Badamasi Babangida (IBB) -- a military dictator and northern Muslim -- introduced reforms to make Local Government Areas (LGAs) more autonomous and democratic. At this time he also divided Jos LGA -- where the Hausa-Fulani Muslim "settlers" were a growing minority. The division created Jos North LGA, where the Hausa-Fulani Muslims were a majority and able to "use their number in a democracy to mitigate vulnerability."[11] The Christian ethnic Berom "indigenes" saw the creation of Jos North LGA as a deliberate strategy to advance the Muslim Hausa-Fulani, especially as Jos North LGA incorporated Jos metropolis. [12]

In February 1999, Nigeria held democratic elections, ending 33 years of military rule mostly by northern Muslims. When Olusegun Obasanjo, a southern Christian, emerged the victor with 63 percent of what was largely accepted as a free and fair vote, northern Muslim powerbrokers were incensed. To maintain influence, the

---

[10] *ECOWAS agrees to Mali intervention force*, 11 November 2012
http://www.aljazeera.com/news/africa/2012/11/20121111192710305682.html

[11] Dr. Aliyu U. Tilde, *The Plateau Crucible (part 2)*, 18 Feb 2010

[12] Elizabeth Kendal *Nigeria: Why is Jos such a tinderbox?* 9 March 2012
http://elizabethkendal.blogspot.com.au/2010/03/nigeria-why-is-jos-such-tinderbox.html

northern governors reinvented themselves as religious reformers. Sharia swept the north.

The northern states' adoption of Islamic Sharia law was unconstitutional and should have been nipped in the bud -- but it wasn't. Subsequently, Islamic zeal escalated and with it, violent persecution. Furthermore, with two conflicting legal codes now in force, Sharia enforcers were perpetually clashing with police, putting Islamic fundamentalists on a collision course with the secular state, fueling the Muslim sense of persecution and victimhood.

This was the context in which **Boko Haram** emerged.

Also known as *Jamaatul Alissunna lid da'a wa wal jihad* and the "Nigerian Taliban", Boko Haram was founded in Maiduguri, Borno State, in 2002 by Sheikh Mohammed Yusuf. His immediate concern was local: the enforcement of Sharia in Borno. But as vigilante Sharia-enforcers, Boko Haram constantly found themselves in conflict with local police enforcing Nigerian common law.

On 26 July 2009, some 150 Boko Haram rampaged through Maiduguri. They attacked the police station, killing police. They attacked the prison, killing guards and liberating prisoners. On 28 July 09, the military responded and by the end of the day more than 780 mostly Boko Haram lay dead in the streets. On 30 July 2009, Boko Haram leader Sheikh Mohammed Yusuf was arrested. The next day, Yusuf was dead in custody.

On 9 August 2009, Boko Haram proclaimed Yusuf and some 1000 dead Islamists "martyrs" and declared *"Jihad in Nigeria"*.

In mid 2010, Boko Haram formalised ties with **al-Qaeda in the Islamic Maghreb (AQIM)**[13] and analysts warned that the game was about to change.

On 13 June 2011, Nigeria experienced its first ever suicide bombing when a Boko Haram militant posing as a police recruit drove his car into Police Headquarters in Abuja and detonated, killing eight. On 26 August 2011, a Boko Haram militant detonated in a car parked outside the UN Headquarters in Abuja, killing twenty-three.

---

[13] Elizabeth Kendal *Nigeria: the Boko Haram threat*, 10 July 2011
http://elizabethkendal.blogspot.com.au/2011/07/nigeria-and-boko-haram-threat.html

As security increased, Boko Haram turned its attentions to softer targets: bars, markets, police stations, court houses, universities, schools, anti-Salafi mosques and churches – mostly across the north.

The terror is putting a strain on national unity and immense pressure on the government of President Goodluck Jonathan. Dozens of churches have been attacked by suicide bombers and gunmen. Dozens of pastors have been murdered, hundreds of Christians have been killed and many thousands displaced.

Ben Kwashi, the Archbishop of Jos, recently told a Melbourne audience that every Sunday morning Christians will ponder the detours, the long waits at numerous check points, the long walks (when you are forced to park a mile down the road) and the risks, and wonder if it is worth it! Josiah Fearon, bishop in Kaduna blames the insecurity for a 30 percent fall in attendance and a 60 percent fall in financial giving. [14]

Today, **Boko Haram**, which now officially linked to **AQIM** – which is operating freely in the Sahel with air-bases in Nth Mali, is inciting and assisting **Fulani** expansion through jihad. Consequently, Fulani raids – usually conducted at night – have become more violent and sophisticated.

On 7 July 2012, some 100 Fulani "herdsmen", many wearing black fatigues and bulletproof vests and armed with assault rifles, descended on nine ethnic Berom Christian villages simultaneously in Barkin Ladi LGA (adjoins Jos South LGA). Sixty-three Berom villagers were killed outright – shot and butchered, – and more than sixty homes were burned.

The next day, as hundreds attended a mass funeral, Fulani gunmen attacked the funeral procession, killing a further twenty-two. Evidence of complicity by rogue military includes reports that military vehicles were deliberately positioned to block access to police and ambulances.

A further fifty bodies were subsequently discovered in the home of a Church of Christ in Nigeria (COCIN) pastor. The victims had been killed the day before (7 July) while escaping Fulani terror. Fleeing to the COCIN church, they were received by the pastor who gave

---

[14] *Bishop laments 30% drop in church attendance*, 11 August 2012
http://www.vanguardngr.com/2012/08/bishop-laments-30-drop-in-church-attendance-in-kaduna/

them refuge in his home. When the Fulani got word of it, they surrounded the house and set it on fire.[15]

What can we do??

As strategic analyst Gregory Copley notes, though geography, environment and politics all are important factors in every situation, the real dynamic element is human.[16]

Praise God for the Gospel, for people *will* beat their swords into ploughshares when they are transformed by Jesus Christ (Isaiah 2:2-4). And the battle *can* be turned back through the LORD of hosts who gives *strength to those who turn back the battle at the gate* (Isaiah 28:5-6).

As such, mission and prayer will remain the most important response, even to these complex, seemingly overwhelming situations. *"For we wrestle not against flesh and blood . . ."*[17]

---

[15] *Nigeria: terror in Plateau State.* Religious Liberty Prayer Bulletin (RLPB) 168, 18 July 2012
http://rlprayerbulletin.blogspot.com.au/2012/07/nigeria-terror-in-plateau-state.html

[16] Gregory R Copley *Strategic Policy in an Age of Global Realignment*, Editor Defense & Foreign Affairs Strategic Policy. 5-6, 2012

[17] See Ephesians 6:10-18

The Causes and Roots of Religious Persecution[1]

Dr Andy Bannister

Adjunct Research Fellow
CSIOF, MST

Introduction: Dying to Make a Difference

Dr. John Joseph was the Catholic Bishop of Faisalabad in Pakistan and a prominent human rights activist. On 6 May 1998, he travelled from his home to the city of Sahiwal to address a prayer meeting being held for victims of blasphemy cases. In Pakistan, the notorious 295-C law makes insulting Muhammad or the Qur'an a crime punishable by death. The law is often used to falsely accuse religious minorities, especially Christians,[2] and Dr. Joseph was concerned about one Christian in particular, Ayub Masih. Arrested in 1996 for allegedly violating the blasphemy laws, Ayub Masih had been held in solitary confinement in a tiny cell, denied medical care, and frequently abused. In April 1998, he had been formally found guilty and had been sentenced to death. After addressing the prayer meeting, Dr. Joseph made his way to the courthouse to the spot where, during the trial, somebody had shot at Ayub Masih and tried to assassinate him. At about 9:30pm, Dr. Joseph took a pistol and took his own life. In a letter to a local newspaper, published after his death, he had written: "dedicated persons do not count the cost of the sacrifices they have to make".[3]

Bishop John Joseph wanted to draw attention to the dire situation facing Pakistan's two million Christians. Everything else had been tried, but the international community seemed deaf to their plight.

---

[1] A longer version of this paper was formally presented at a Parliamentary Forum on Religious Persecution, Ottawa, Monday 21 March 2011.

[2] See David G. Littman and René Wadlow, 'Blasphemy legislation in Pakistan's Penal Code', United Nations Economic and Social Council, 14 July 1998, http://www.unhchr.ch/Huridocda/Huridoca.nsf/0/7531e0f1f0b77ce480256657 0035e7f5 (accessed 20 March 2011).

[3] BBC News 7 May 1998, 'Despatches: Karachi': http://news.bbc.co.uk/2/hi/south_asia/88890.stm (accessed 19 March 2011).

Frustrated, he concluded that only something so dramatic as his taking his own life would effect any change.[4]

Sadly, it seems that his hope was misplaced. Although the international community is now more aware than ever of religious persecution,[5] the situation is still bleak. It is presently estimated that some 200 million Christians in 60 countries live under daily threat of persecution. Between 2008 and 2009, 176,000 were killed. Some estimate that if nothing is done, then by 2025, an average of 210,000 Christians will be being killed each year.[6] Asma Jahangir, the UN Special Rapporteur on Religious Freedom or Belief wrote:

> [Discrimination] based on religion or belief preventing individuals from fully enjoying all their human rights still occurs worldwide on a daily basis.[7]

Launching its 2011 annual report on religious freedom worldwide, the Catholic charity, Aid to the Church in Need, concluded that 75% of all religious persecution in the world is currently directed at Christian minorities. At the launch, Archbishop Warda of Erbil in Iraq spoke about the difficulties in his country:

> We wonder if we will survive as a people in our own country[8] ... The past is terrifying, the present is not promising.[9]

---

[4] Ayub Masih was finally released, five years after his arrest: See 'Religious Prisoner Profile: Ayub Masih (Pakistan)', *Religious Prisoners Congressional Task Force*, http://www.house.gov/pitts/initiatives/humanrights/prisoners/masih. htm (accessed 19 March 2011).

[5] For example, in 1998 the United States passed the International Religious Freedom Act, mandating the US State Department to publish an annual report tracking religious freedom in some two hundred countries around the world. Much of the data is available online at http://www.thearda.com/.

[6] Figures from the World Evangelical Alliance. See http://www.m-b-t.org/2010/03/25/how-many-christians-are-killed-for-their-faith-every-year/. See also '200 million Christians in 60 countries subject to persecution', Catholic News Agency (19 June 2007) http://www.catholicnewsagency.com/news/200_million_christians_in_60_countries_subject_to_persecution/

[7] Asma Jahangir, "Report of the Special Rapporteur on Freedom of Religion or Belief", Human Rights Council, Tenth Session, Item 3.

8 Terry Murphy, 'New report reveals 75 percent of religious persecution is against Christians, *Aid to the Church In Need* 16 March 2001, http://www.acnuk.org/news.php/205/ukinternational-new-report-reveals-75-percent-of-religious-persecution-is-against-christians (accessed 19 March 2011).

[9] Time is Running Out for Iraq's Christians, Says Archbishop', *Assyrian International News Agency*, 19 March 2011, http://www.aina.org/news/20110318234137.htm (accessed 20 March 2011).

More than half the Christians in Iraq have fled. A community once numbering over a million is now down to about 150,000.

Where is Persecution Happening?

All of this is deeply troubling. But *why* is this happening? Can we identify any patterns to religious persecution across the globe, any causes or trends that might help us formulate a response?

The answer to that question is yes. But let's begin by taking a step back and asking *where* precisely it is that religious persecution is happening. Whilst persecution is a global phenomena, there are patterns that we can track.

Brian Grim and Roger Finke, two sociologists who have produced some of the most recent analyses of religious persecution, have used a number of studies to answer this very question: where is persecution happening. Their figures look like this:[10]

	Muslim Majority	Other Majority (Atheist, Buddhist, Hindu, Jewish)	No Religion with More than 50%	Christian Majority	World Average
>200 abused or displaced	62%	85%	33%	28%	43%

If we look at even higher rates of persecution, the differences are also striking:

> Persecution of more than one thousand persons is present in 45 percent of Muslim-majority countries and 60 percent of the "Other Majority" religion countries, compared to 11 percent of Christian-majority countries and 8 percent of countries where no single religion holds a majority.[11]

These figures are consistently backed up by other studies. For example, the 2011 Open Doors "World Watch List" listed 51

---

[10] Grim and Finke, *The Price of Freedom Denied*, 21.

[11] Ibid., 22.

countries of concern: 65% were Muslim-majority countries.[12] Of the top ten human rights offenders, seven were Muslim-majority and two were communist atheistic states.[13]

What could be the cause of these kind of figures? One common denominator, whether the country in which the persecution is occurring is Muslim or atheist, Hindu, Buddhist, or no-majority-religion — is *religious regulation*. There is a direct correlation between attempts by a state to control, regulate or restrict religious activity and religious persecution. Restriction on or regulation of religion is a surprisingly common phenomena. According to the Pew Forum:

> [N]early 70 percent of the world's 6.8 billion people live in countries with high restrictions on religion, the brunt of which often falls on religious minorities.[14]

There are two ways that a state can attempt to control religious activity or restrict religious freedom within its borders. First, a government can use the full force of the state, for example by passing laws, arresting or harassing worshippers or religious leaders. So, for example, in China, the communist government regularly marks the start of Lent by bulldozing churches and rounding up Christians to remind them of the consequences of daring to be a religious believer in the officially atheistic People's Republic.[15]

As well as using the apparatus of the state, a government can also encourage or allow social pressure build up to make it hard for the members of a minority religious community to practice their faith. On 4 January last year, the governor of Punjab province, Salman Taseer, was getting into his car at a market when one of his own bodyguards opened fire and shot him 26 times. Why? The bodyguard was angry that Mr. Taseer was opposed to Pakistan's blasphemy law and had appealed for the pardon of a Christian

---

[12] 'Open Doors 2011 World Watch List Top 10 Focus', http://www.opendoorsca.org/images/homepage/wwwltopten.pdf (accessed 19 March 2011).

[13] The Muslim-majority states listed were Iran, Afghanistan, Saudi Arabia, Somalia, the Maldives, Yemen and Iraq. The two communist, atheist states were North Korea and Laos. (The tenth country they listed was Uzbekistan).

[14] Global Restrictions on Religion', 17 Dec 2010, http://pewforum.org/Government/Global-Restrictions-on-Religion. aspx (accessed 20 March 2011).

[15] Brett M. Decker, 'Beijing's Fear of Faith', *The Washington Times*, 14 March 2011, http://www.washingtontimes.com/ news/2011/mar/14/decker-beijings-fear-faith/ (accessed 19 March 2011).

woman, Asia Bibi, who had been sentenced to death for allegedly insulting Muhammad.[16]

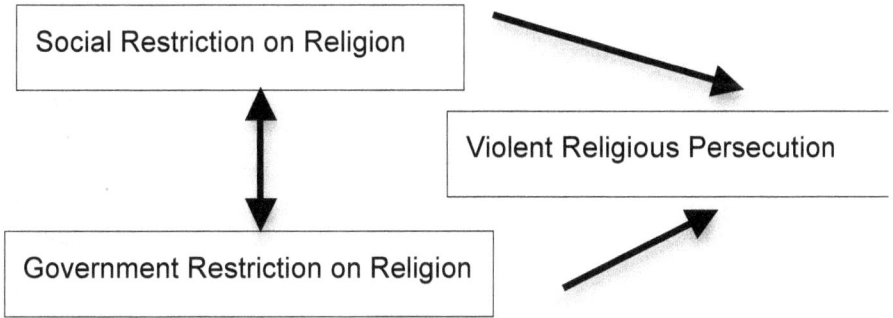

```
┌─────────────────────────────────┐
│  Social Restriction on Religion │ ──────┐
└─────────────────────────────────┘       │
          ↕                         ┌──────────────────────────────┐
┌─────────────────────────────────┐│  Violent Religious Persecution│
│Government Restriction on Religion│└──────────────────────────────┘
└─────────────────────────────────┘ ──────┘
```

Those two stories illustrate the way that social pressures and government pressures on religious minorities work together and cause persecution. If the Pakistan government had the courage to remove the 295-C blasphemy law, this would remove much of the fuel from the fire that popular Islamist movements are trying to light.

How Do You Solve a Problem Like Sharia?

This connection between social restrictions, government restrictions and violent religious persecution begins to help explain the extremely high rate of religious persecution in Muslim-majority countries. Built into Islam is a ready-made system of religious law, *Sharia*.[17] Because a whole codified body of religious law is readily available, governments in Muslim-majority countries face an ever present temptation to draw upon or incorporate aspects of Sharia into their legal systems.

Those that have resisted the temptation are facing a growing popular pressure to do so. A 2006 Gallup survey of ten Muslim-

[16] 'Punjab Governor Salman Taseer assassinated in Islamabad', BBC News Online, 4 January 2011, http://www.bbc.co.uk/news/world-south-asia-12111831 (accessed 19 March 2011). See also Mohammed Hanif, 'How Pakistan responded to Salmaan Taseer's assassination', *The Guardian*, 6 January 2011, http://www. guardian.co.uk/world/2011/jan/06/pakistan-salman-taseer-assassination (accessed 19 March 2011). A few months later, another politician, Shahbaz Bhatti, the Minority Affairs Minister and the only Christian in Pakistan's cabinet, was gunned down, again because of his well-publicised opposition to the blasphemy laws

[17] An excellent introduction to and survey of *Sharia* law is Joseph Schacht, *Introduction to Islamic Law* (Oxford: Oxford University Press, 1964).

majority countries found that 79% wanted *Sharia* in *some* form.[18] Indeed, 66% of Egyptians and 60% of Pakistanis said they wanted *Sharia* as the *only* source of legislation. [19] Even an astonishing 40% of British Muslims said they wanted *Sharia*.[20]

Apostasy and Blasphemy Laws

Sharia law is a problem because many of its stipulations have tremendous implications for religious minorities. Perhaps the two biggest issues are apostasy and blasphemy. All four main schools of *Sharia* treat apostasy and blasphemy as very serious offences, often punishable by death. That presents a huge problem for freedom of religious belief.

In 1998, Lina Joy, a Malay Muslim woman, declared she wished to become a Christian. However, in Malaysia, your identity card carries your religion. Bravely she applied to have it changed from "Muslim" to "Christian". The government refused and said she would need an "Apostasy Certificate" from a *Sharia* Court. The government lawyer said:

> If you are born Muslim, you stay Muslim, at least until a *Sharia* court decides otherwise, which is never.[21]

There was a further problem too. If Lina Joy *did* go to a *Sharia* court, she would run the risk of criminal punishment as an apostate — for which the penalty could be death. Wan Azhar Wan Ahmad, Senior Fellow at the Institute of Islamic Understanding said:

> If Islam were to grant permission for Muslims to change religion at will, it would imply it has no dignity, no self-

---

[18] A 2007 University of Maryland poll found similar figures. See Toni Johnson and Lauren Vriens, 'Islam: Governing Under Sharia', *Council on Foreign Relations*, 10 Nov 2010, http://www.cfr.org/religion/islam-governing-under-sharia/p8034 (accessed 19 March 2011).

[19] Dalia Mogahed, 'Islam and Democracy', Gallup World Poll, http://media.gallup.com/MuslimWestFacts/PDF/ GALLUPMUSLIMSTUDIESIslamandDemocracy030607rev.pdf (accessed 19 March 2011). The study found the rates for Jordan were 54% and for Bangladesh, 52%.

[20] Patrick Hennessy and Melissa Kite, 'Poll Reveals 40pc of Muslims want Sharia Law in UK, *The Telegraph*, 19 Feb 2006, http://www.telegraph.co.uk/news/uknews/1510866/Poll-reveals-40pc-of-Muslims-want-sharia-law-in-UK.html (accessed 19 March 2011).

[21] Doug Bandow, 'The Right Not to be a Muslim', *National Review Online*, 8 June 2007, http://www.nationalreview.com/articles/221155/right-not-be-muslim/doug-bandow (accessed 19 March 2011).

esteem. And people may then question its completeness, truthfulness and perfection.[22]

Lina Joy was disowned by her family and lost her job. She was unable to marry her boyfriend, a Catholic, since under *Sharia* law, a Muslim woman cannot marry a non-Muslim. She and her fiancé were forced into hiding after Muslim extremists threatened to kill them.[23]

In December 2010, the Pew Forum conducted a survey to ascertain what Muslims around the world thought about *Sharia*-based laws, such as apostasy. In Egypt, 84% approved of the death sentence for apostasy. In Pakistan it was 76%, Jordan 86% and even in Indonesia it was 30%.[24]

Things are as difficult for religious minorities when we turn from apostasy to blasphemy. We have already seen how Pakistan has woven this into its criminal code with the 295-C Blasphemy Law, which is often used to target religious minorities. In June 2009, Asia Bibi, an agricultural worker in a rural village in Pakistan drank some water from her village well. Local Muslims complained, saying Christians were "unclean" and so the water was now polluted. An argument ensued. A few days later, villagers claimed that during the argument, Asia Bibi had insulted Muhammad. A mob turned up at her home, beating her and family, before the police rescued her then promptly charged her with blasphemy. She spent a year in prison before, in November 2010, she was sentenced to death by hanging.[25]

History and Theology Collide

In their study of contemporary religious persecution, Brian Grim and Roger Finke note that a major problem in tackling these issues is that religion is often ignored in studies of social unrest, subsumed

---

[22] Ibid.

[23] 'Malaysia rejects Christian appeal', *BBC News Online*, 30 May 2007, http://news.bbc.co.uk/2/hi/asia-pacific/6703155.stm (accessed 19 March 2011).

[24] See 'Muslim Publics Divided on Hamas and Hezbollah', *Pew Research Center*, 2 Dec 2010, http://pewglobal.org/2010/12/02/muslims-around-the-world-divided-on-hamas-and-hezbollah/ (accessed 19 March 2011).

[25] Rob Crilly and Aoun Sahi, 'Christian woman sentenced to death in Pakistan "for blasphemy"', *The Telegraph*, 9 Nov 2010, http://www.telegraph.co.uk/news/religion/8120142/Christian-woman-sentenced-to-death-in-Pakistan-for-blasph emy.html (accessed 19 March 2011). See also Declan Walsh, 'Salmaan Taseer, Aasia Bibi and Pakistan's struggle with extremism', *The Guardian*, 8 Jan 2011, http://www.guardian.co.uk/world/2011/jan/08/salmaan-taseer-blasphemy-pakistan-bibi (accessed 19 March 2011).

under "ethnicity" or "culture".[26] Many academics, journalists and politicians have bought into what, for simplicity's sake, one might label the "Marxist view of religion". Rather than take religion seriously, everything is explained in social or economic terms.[27] The problem is that if you do that, you will misrepresent the seriousness of religious persecution today, and fail to understand its prevalence in Muslim-majority countries and its connection with *Sharia*.

The Way Forward

Religious rights don't exist in a vacuum but are connected to other fundamental human rights. The right to freedom of belief is connected to the right to freedom of expression. The right to freedom of worship is connected to the right to freedom of assembly. Where religious rights are being suppressed, you can be sure that other fundamental human rights are too. Freedom of religion and religious persecution are litmus tests for other human rights abuses.[28]

What can be done? Most importantly, the problem needs to be brought into the open. There are signs this is beginning to happen. Canada is just about to launch it's new Office of Religious Freedom within the Department of Foreign Affairs.[29] Whilst a leader article in *The Economist* recently bravely opined that:

> There is a specific problem with Islam. Islamic law (though not the Koran) has often mandated death for people leaving the faith ... [M]ore Muslim leaders need to accept that changing creed is a legal right. On that one point, the West

---

[26] Brian J. Grim and Roger Finke, 'Religious Persecution in Cross-National Context: Clashing Civilizations or Regulated Religious Economies?', *American Sociological Review* 72.4 (2007) 633-658, citing 633.

[27] It is ironic that the so called "New Atheists" such as Richard Dawkins and Christopher Hitchens swing entirely the *other* direction and say that religion is the *only* cause of most social ills. See e.g. David Bentley Hart, *Atheist Delusions: The Christian Revolution and Its Fashionable Enemies* (London: Yale University Press, 2009) for a critique.

[28] See also Marshall, 'The Range of Religious Freedom in 2008', 28 for a critique of the suggestion that religious rights are a luxury only to be worried about once "basic needs" such as food and shelter have been obtained.

[29] Steve Chase, 'Conservatives laying groundwork for Office of Religious Freedom' (*The Globe and Mail*, 1 Jan 2012) http://www.theglobeandmail.com/news/politics/conservatives-laying-groundwork-for-office-of-religious-freedom/article2288479/?utm_medium=Feeds%3A%20RSS%2FAtom&utm_source=Politics&utm_content=2288479 (Accessed 6 Jan 2012).

should not back down. Otherwise believers, whether Christian or not, remain in peril.[30]

Jesus said: "Everyone who does evil hates the light, and does not come to the light, lest their deeds should be exposed" (John 3:20). We need to expose and talk about the issue of religious persecution. The victims demand it. Their blood cries out.

---

[30] 'Christians and Lions' (The Economist, 31 Dec 2011)
http://www.economist.com/node/21542195 (Accessed 6 Jan 2012)

"Innocence of Muslims": Taking Stock of Muslim Protests

Dr Peter Riddell

What does Pope Benedict XVI have in common with a bunch of cartoons from Denmark and a Z-grade movie trailer produced in Southern California? Answer: all have triggered riots of Muslims around the world, being deemed to have impugned the reputation of Muhammad, prophet of Islam.

The Pope's 2006 speech at Regensberg in which he quoted a medieval Byzantine Emperor's negative comment about Muhammad, and the cartoons of Muhammad published in the Danish newspaper *Jyllands-Posten* in September 2005, have now passed into the annals of history. At the time of writing the impact of the 14 minute film trailer *Innocence of Muslims*, uploaded to Youtube in mid-2012, appears to be headed in the same direction. But there is little doubt that another such event will take place in coming years. So it is of value to examine key issues relating to the film trailer so that next time we are better prepared for Muslim outrage.

The author and producer of *Innocence of Muslims*[1] is reportedly a 55 year old Coptic Christian, Nakoula Basseley Nakoula, who lives near Los Angeles. As a Copt he would have an axe to grind, given the ongoing plight of the Coptic minority in Muslim-majority Egypt. But Nakoula may be of questionable integrity in his own right. In late September 2012 he was arrested by US federal authorities for violating the terms of probation related to earlier periods in jail.

With regard to the trailer itself, criticism has not only come from Muslims. Indeed, most of the film's cast have dissociated themselves from it, angry that references to Islam were dubbed over the original script after the filming. But there is an "elephant in the room", according to Christian debater Jay Smith. He argues that of the 20 scenes in the trailer, 17 of them draw their information,

---

[1] The trailer is available at http://www.youtube.com/watch?v=mjoa3QazVy8

directly or indirectly, from Islamic literature, including the Qur'an itself.[2]

A close examination of the trailer scenes bears out Smith's claim, but also in some cases identifies an intention to offend on the part of the film producer. For example, Qur'an verse 93:6 refers to Muhammad being an orphan. Some non-Muslim writing suggests uncertainty regarding the identity of Muhammad's father; an early scene in the trailer engages with this in a sensationalist way by referring to him repeatedly as "the bastard".

Similarly, the intimate scene in the tent between Khadija and Muhammad draws on the original biography of Muhammad, as well as Bukhari's Hadith collection,[3] but depicts these accounts in a more licentious way than in the biography and the traditions.

However, some scenes present a controversial angle on the prophet of Islam without any basis in Islamic literature. The suggestion that Muhammad was gay in one scene is not supported by the Islamic literature and seems designed simply to inflame Muslim opinion.

On the other hand, some scenes draw on the Islamic materials faithfully. The scenes that depict Muhammad involved in warfare are strongly attested in the biographical literature as well as in the Qur'an itself. Furthermore, the 13th scene of the trailer depicts the child Aisha being given over in marriage to the 53 year old Muhammad by her father. This is attested in many references in both Bukhari's collection of traditions[4] and the original biography of Muhammad.

So if at least some of the movie's claims can be grounded in Islamic literature, what lies behind the widespread Muslim protests? While many non-Muslim commentators see a bigger agenda than the film, Daniel Pipes reminds readers that the film is a significant factor in the Muslim reaction. "Rage directed at the video was heartfelt, real, and persistent," he writes. "The person of Muhammad has acquired a saint-like quality among Muslims and may not be criticized, much less mocked."[5]

---

[2] See Smith's detailed discussion at http://www.youtube.com/watch?v=N5DGzmsQ470

[3] *Sahih Bukhari* 1:3 and 96:1-3.

[4] *Sahih al-Bukhari* 7:64, 88 etc.

[5] http://www.danielpipes.org/11994/muhammad-protests-post-mortem

This is no doubt true. For millions of Muslims, Muhammad is exemplar, and mockery of that exemplar is keenly felt. Indeed, his role as a model for Muslim behavior can even be seen in the violent reactions to the film. A commentator called Khaled points out on the *answering-islam.org* website that Muhammad's response to insult was unambiguous: "Muhammad ordered a few people to be executed wherever they could be found, even in the sacred space of the Kaaba where nobody should be hurt. It is interesting to see that most of those who he ordered to be killed were people who insulted him."[6]

However, viewing the landscape of the *Innocence of Muslims* issue is like looking at a Bruegel painting. If one stands up close a lot of detail is available, but if one looks from afar a big picture is discernible. In the case of the film, that big picture relates to a persistent campaign by Muslim nations to push for anti-blasphemy legislation throughout the world designed to eliminate criticism of Islam.

Elizabeth Kendal suggests that the 'Cartoon Intifada' of February 2006 was intended to apply pressure to a meeting of the UN Human Rights Commission,[7] with this body adopting resolutions about the defamation of religion on a number of occasions. She further notes the recent statement by Professor Dr. Ahmad at-Tayyib, Grand Sheikh of al-Azhar in Cairo, linking the Muslim reaction to the film *Innocence of Muslims* with a need for anti-blasphemy legislation by the UN. Dr. at-Tayyib writes: "Al-Azhar ... addresses U.N. Secretary-General Mr. Ban Ki-moon... It is now high time for a resolution that criminalize [sic] defamation of Islamic figures, and the figures of all other world religions, given that the attack against them disturbs world peace and threatens international security."[8]

This larger agenda by Muslim lobby groups is likely to encounter two significant hurdles. The first relates to the First Amendment of the U.S. Constitution that has been regularly upheld by the US Supreme Court for over seventy years as invalidating government restrictions on blasphemy and hate speech. This position on hate

---

[6] http://answering-islam.org/authors/khaled/movie2.html

[7] http://rlprayerbulletin.blogspot.com.au/2012/09/film-riots-praying-through-crisis.html

[8] http://www.onislam.net/english/shariah/muhammad/misconceptions/459054-statement-of-al-azhar-ash-sharif-on-the-qfilmq-.html

speech was reiterated by the Supreme Court by an 8-1 majority in March 2011.[9]

The second major hurdle which will galvanise opposition in the West to the push for anti-blasphemy legislation relates to a clear case of double standards on the part of Muslim activists. As eloquently put by Elizabeth Kendal, "the film is far less offensive than much of the anti-Christian material that offends, hurts and sickens Christians -- who do not riot."[10]

---

[9] http://en.wikipedia.org/wiki/Innocence_of_Muslims

[10] http://rlprayerbulletin.blogspot.com.au/2012/09/film-riots-praying-through-crisis.html

Communiqués

The Leonard Buck Lecture in Missiology, 5 May 2012 "Do Christians and Muslims worship the same God?"

The 2012 Leonard Buck Lecture in Missiology addressed a topic that is receiving much attention within the broader Church in Australia and overseas. The speaker was to be Dr John Azumah, Associate Professor of World Christianity and Islam at Columbia Theological Seminary in Atlanta, Georgia. Unfortunately, Dr Azumah was forced to withdraw due to serious family illness. In his place, the topic was addressed by three speakers: Dr Mark Durie, prominent scholar and author and Chairman of the CSIOF Advisory Board; and Dr Peter Riddell and Dr Bernie Power of the CSIOF.

Mark began the evening with a presentation of fundamental questions that underlie the issue of a common God across religions. In his concise and lucid talk, the audience was shown that it was no simple matter to conclude that different religions worshipped the same God.

Peter Riddell then devoted his talk to a summary of the arguments of Prof. Miroslav Volf whose recent book, *Allah: A Christian Response*, argues for a common God across Christianity and Islam. Prof. Volf's arguments take account of wide ranging historical, theological and sociological factors.

In response, Bernie Power presented his arguments against the common God approach. In the process he questioned the view that a common God would help Christian-Muslim relations, pointing to examples from history which showed bitter conflict between groups which seemingly worshipped a common God. He went on to scrutinize theological factors relating to Islam's monotheism and the Trinitarian understanding of Christianity, concluding that differences in the understanding of God between Islam and Christianity were fundamental.

The audience of 200 were actively engaged during the 30 minutes of question time, showing that the topic being addressed was seen as relevant to the modern Church, and suggesting that the arguments both for and against had been lucidly presented. The evening's discussion was followed by a supper, providing a further opportunity for discussion in small groups around the topic of the evening.

Faith and Culture Lectures

In June 2012, Melbourne's Wheeler Centre held a week of lectures entitled *Faith and Culture: The Politics of Belief*, comprising lectures and panel discussions examining the relationship of religion to politics and society. Two seminars were given by Muslim speakers: prominent British Muslim sociologist, Tariq Modood, and Director of the Center for the Study of Culture, Race and Ethnicity at Ithaca College, New York, Asma Barlas.

Tariq Modood is an academic and researcher on ethnic minorities who regularly contributes to the British media and promotes a "multiculturalism of hope." He gave an informative analysis of the interaction between Secular Humanism and religion in Western Europe. He correctly identified a reduction in Christian Churches' engagement with politics in the last half century, while minority religions, and especially Islam have in recent years sought an increasing involvement with public policy. Essentially, just as secularism reached a peak, Muslims and others have challenged this idea. Some sociologists have started to speak about a post-secular society, partly because of the emergence of political Islam in the West.

Modood states that governments now recognise religious affiliation as a category alongside categories like race and gender. In the past someone was "Indian", but their self-identity as "Muslim" is also important. Modood also argues that it's important to understand and address the disadvantages of groups like Muslims as part of his conception of multi-cultural citizenship. All Western European countries have secular governments, though in differing degrees. Despite this secularism, most countries still see religion as a public good, and some even publicly fund State Churches.

In the late 1980s, the publishing of *The Satanic Verses* and the banning of head scarves by a French high school principal highlighted the tensions between governments and Muslims. The British Government was never going to ban Salman Rushdie's work, and the protests calling for this exposed a gap in understanding. Since then, Muslims have lobbied governments regarding their own issues which has led to increased contact between politicians and Muslim leaders. One response from British Prime Minister David Cameron is a call for "muscular liberalism" which allows religious identification, but not in opposition to national identification. Ultimately though, Muslim populations are increasing in the West and politicians need to find ways to work with Muslims (and others) to reduce tensions in a multi-cultural society.

In contrast to Modood's relatively measured approach, Asma Barlas launched straight into an assault on the West for perceived attacks on Muslims. Barlas traced the history of Western literature's view of Muhammad as "Antichrist", explaining that Muslims have always been seen as "the other" and misunderstood by Western society. She criticised the terrifying depiction of Muslims in medieval literature without acknowledging the genuine fear of Islamic armies advancing against Europe.

There were references to recent Western depictions of Islam such as the Danish cartoons and Dutch film maker Theo Van Gogh's film *Submission* (for which he was murdered by a Muslim), but in the end, the lecture made little sense. A strong denunciation of the West should be backed up by some hard evidence, not a couple of controversial events that don't represent the West's overall view of Islam. Bernie Power of MST asked Barlas why she was so selective and warned her that her anti-Western views could see her convicted under Religious Vilification legislation in Victoria. His question received applause from a portion of the audience.

The two reports were very different in style. Modood used many statistics and presented as someone sharing interesting information for the audience to consider. Barlas went on the offensive and tried to get the audience to examine their guilt over negative views of Muslims. It is a fact that the Muslim populations of Western Europe and countries like Australia are increasing. Modood's analysis was that all groups should be involved in the political process, but he didn't cover some of the more difficult issues such as a push for *Sharia* law or whether Islam is compatible with democracy (a question asked by Bernie Power but not answered satisfactorily). Muslims have become more vocal in stating their views, but there seems no clear answer about whether Islam can co-exist with Western democracy. Modood reminded the audience that in the past the Catholic Church had a problem with democracy, but didn't point out that unlike Christianity, Islam has scriptural imperatives which drive government structure.

Ironically, Barlas' seminar about how Westerners misunderstand Islam was more likely to alienate than bring understanding. Perhaps those who already feel a heavy guilt for the West's relationship with Islam may have rallied around her, but I couldn't relate at all.

It is very interesting to see how Muslims choose to address a non-Muslim audience. Neither speaker aimed to convert their audience to Islam, but both should have been seeking to win their audience to their point of view. Modood spoke interestingly and informatively about how Muslims interact with Western society. Barlas spoke scathingly and unhelpfully about how Muslims are viewed in the West. Both contribute to the debate, but Modood is very well known and respected, even if he had less people at his seminar on this occasion.

J S Leslie
Post Graduate Student
MST

EUSEBIA School of Theology

As part of our support to promote the spread of the Gospel of Christ in Islamic contexts and to strengthen Christian converts from various religious backgrounds in their new faith, we have developed theological courses which focus specifically on these issues.

For this purpose we are planning to conduct our second *Graduate Seminar in Theology (GST)* in Stuttgart/Germany. This GST is designed to provide Master's level education to students who have already completed their Bachelor's degree in theology.

The aim of the GST is to develop awareness of the Biblical-Semitic understanding of the Bible in Western Theology on the one hand and to focus on how to convey the truth of the Gospel to the Muslim understanding which is confined to the Semitic concept of the Qur'an, on the other.

Our faculty consists of four lecturers with international and intercultural experience who will teach modules in the areas of Old Testament, Biblical Theology, Systematic Theology and Biblical Hermeneutics. We expect to have four to six students from various countries.

Literary Aspects of Old Testament Research

Our Ministry has conducted its sixth symposium (or expert conference) for Bible, Theology and Missions in October 2011 in Stuttgart, Germany. The conference papers are now published in the volume STUTTGARTER THEOLOGISCHE THEMEN both in German and English language.

The conference took place under the title: *"Literary Structures of Old Testament Texts and their Significance for the Biblical-Semitic Understanding of God's Revelation"*

The focus of this conference was on the literary aspects of the Old Testament which have been largely neglected in Western theological scholarship. However, the literary structures of the Hebrew text of the Old Testament are essential to perceive and demonstrate their relevance for our understanding of the text.

Particularly in light of the affinity between the Hebrew and other Semitic languages, such as Arabic, and other thought structures as well, this "Biblical-Semitic approach" proves fruitful for the constructive interaction and dialogue with contemporary Islam.

Therefore the main speaker at this symposium was the eminent literary scholar Dr. Meir Sternberg, Professor of Literature at Tel Aviv University. He expounded two historical narrative texts, namely 1 Kings 1-2 and Genesis 23. In both texts he highlighted the presence and significance of two foundational literary laws of the Hebrew Bible. These are the *law of indirection* and the *law of omission*. Through these laws the two levels of the written, explicit text and the unwritten, implicit assumptions before the text, are interrelated. Only if the reader connects these two levels of reading, will he understand properly the purpose of the author and the intended meaning for the reader.

The previous conference volumes are available online at www.sttonline.org

Dr Markus Piennisch,
Director of theological studies
Eusebia School of Theology

Reviews

Readers are invited to submit reviews of recent publications on the study of Islam and other faiths for possible inclusion in the CSIOF Bulletin.

Different Angles on Jihad

REUVEN FIRESTONE. *Jihad: The Origin of Holy War in Islam*, New York: Oxford University Press, 1999. xi +195pp. pb.

M. J. AKBAR. *Shade of Swords: Jihad and the Conflict between Islam and Christianity*, London: Routledge, 2002. xx + 272pp. hb.

Jihad and *Shade of Swords* are written by a Jew and a Muslim respectively. Firestone, is a Jewish professor in medieval Judaism and Islam. Akbar, is a prominent Muslim media guru who has had previous experience in national government. On a literary level dissimilarity might be expected; an American scholar and an Asian journalist are likely to express their subject differently not least in their choice of genre. However, their truly divergent treatments of the Islamic concept of *jihad* reflect a wider disparity governed primarily by their methodology and purpose. Whilst Firestone seeks to present a critical, dispassionate study in his analysis of primary sources, Akbar, by contrast, employs an apologetic, polemical tone to commentate on Islam's engagement with 'holy war' and global history.

In *Jihad*, Firestone critically examines the origins and early development of *jihad*. In so doing he questions its actual origins and challenges the notion that the Islamic concept of divinely sanctioned war evolved in a 'consistent and linear manner'. He consistently uses the primary sources of pre-Islamic poetry, the Qur'an and Oral tradition (which are committed to writing in the form of *hadith* (tradition) and *sira* (biography)), to construct a context in which to examine his theme and reconstruct accepted Islamic thought.

Unlike Akbar who pins the origins of jihad to the battle of Badr after the emigration (*hijra*) to Medina, Firestone finds the origins of jihad in the 'mundane' war of the pre-Islamic tribal system. After a short but important chapter explaining the semantic roots of the word *jihad* which need not imply a warring or religious usage, Firestone describes the inter-tribal raiding patterns of pre-Islamic society as an expression of functional, economic and social war. Using pre-Islamic poetry, he shows that these warrings were neither religious nor ideological. The advent of Muhammad's ideological monotheism, however, saw *jihad* 'Islamised' and warring become a 'fight in the path of God'.

Firestone's analysis of relevant Qur'anic passages leads him to suggest a new reading which casts doubt on the accepted 'evolutionary theory' of *jihad*. Based on his understanding that commentaries (*tafsir*) from the first five Islamic centuries which cite occasions of revelation (*asbab al-nuzul*) and abrogations (*naskh*) are often contradictory and unreliable, he concludes that the traditional schema of smooth transition from non-confrontation to defensive fighting to unconditional war may be a retrospective one. Whilst maintaining that the Qur'an is an important primary source he does suggest that the established doctrine of *jihad* may well reflect the 'policy of the empire under which the theory evolved' (p.51). Thus, Firestone interprets the jihadi verses in such a way as to indicate a less than seamless transition. Certain Medinan verses, for example, which talk of the 'People of the Book', still advocate a non-militant approach (Q2: 109; 5:13, 29:46, 42:15). Significant (although suppressed) resistance to warring tendencies in both Meccan and Medinan communities are not completely erased from the Qur'anic script (Q: 2:216, 3:156) and dissonant voices are heard through the verses which address tensions related to various pre-Islamic sacred customs (e.g. the Sacred Months; Q2:194, 9:36). Despite these voices being hushed in the Qur'an and in the *hadith* when oral tradition was committed to written canonical collections they can still be heard with careful exegetical study.

Firestone consequently constructs a picture of communities in transition particularly in the early Medinan period leading up to the battle of Badr. This is further explained through his analysis of biographical *sira* which shows the shifting allegiance and loyalty from tribal kinship group to religious community. Relying largely on Ibn Hisham's ninth century recension of Muhammad bin Ishaq's earlier work, Firestone paints a picture of seventh century Islam as a 'supertribe' increasingly commanding loyalty for a predominantly ideological rather than filial cause. Such an unprecedented shift was bound to cause difficulty and dissent is to be found in the *sira* despite the gloss of editorship.

Firestone's reconstruction, nevertheless, is reliant on traditional chronology at times (which he admits p.132), and his reconstruction does still retain a sense of the linear. The line may not be straight and true but it still moves inexorably forward. Thus he does not present the radical challenge to the evolution of combat and aggression in early Islam first hoped for. This said, he does suggest that the Qur'an, *hadith* and *sira* provide us with a residue of information which suggests reality and outcomes could have been different.

In *Shade of Swords*, Akbar has a far wider scope covering global *jihad* from the seventh century to the present day. The early Meccan-Medinan period covered by Firestone is for Akbar the inspiration for the development of the concept of *jihad* when, against all odds, Muhammad led his army to victory. Badr signifies the essence of holy war; heroism against tyranny, victory against the infidel, martyrdom in battle, defence of faith, hope when all seems lost. Then it 'was the Quraysh....now it is the Christian West' (p.3). Such military triumphs akin to Badr are then celebrated by Akbar as he catalogues the history of *jihad*. From the fall of Constantinople (allegedly foretold by Mohammad in Bukhari's *hadith*), to the military prowess of Saladin in the Crusades, Akbar is quick to attribute success to the 'spirit of Badr' and apparent but temporary failure to lessons learnt from the Battle of Uhud. All defeat is temporary; 'it is only a setback in the holy war' (p.213).

The historical detail and political insight of this book is commendable. Akbar's knowledge of Indian Hindu-Muslim history and the partitioning of Pakistan are enlightening. His views on the need for democracy form a fitting prelude to what has now been termed the 'Arab-Spring'. The book is punctuated with anecdotes and longer narrative which often have a didactic edge. In addition, Akbar's punchy style spares the reader from wading through treacle despite the historical mileage covered. However, some concerns, tensions and omissions may be identified.

Firstly, Akbar appears to adopt a polarised understanding of the concept of *jihad*. Given that he acknowledges, like Firestone, that *jihad* exists in other forms (indeed the internal struggle *Jihad al Akbar* is the greater form), it is unfortunate that he is not willing to consider the possibility that the external struggle, *Jihad al-Asghar*, might have a non-confrontational face. Indeed passive *jihad* for Akbar is something of an oxymoron. He derides those Muslims who 'will convert jihad into a holy bath rather than a holy war' (p.xv). His dismisses Gandhi's non-violent *jihad* as contrary to the Muslim mind-set (p.175) and his apparent unwillingness to consider more conciliatory Sufi views on *jihad* only serves to bear out this point. Thus, the reader's final impression is that *jihad* has been presented from a somewhat narrow perspective.

Secondly, Akbar, unlike Firestone, lacks the critical analysis of the term *jihad* which is required. Yes, he does attempt an exegetical commentary of Sura 2 but despite this, further justification for his usage is in order. Largely absent in his analysis of *jihad* is consideration of *asbab al-nuzul* and *naskh* which are central to Firestone's reading. He does cite Abdullah Yusuf Ali's commentary and an anecdote from *Sahih al-Bukhari* but there is no comparison of views or critical analysis of the text. Little mention is made of *hadith* and *tafsir* which Firestone often refers to in extensive endnotes. Rather Akbar offers us a cursory interpretation of the Qur'an which takes the 'evolutionary theory' at a non-critical face value. In so doing he declares his presuppositional position of understanding Islam to favour war as permissible in self-defence.

This self-positioning enables him to distance himself from terrorism and radical Islamism but his outworking of 'self-defence' lacks perspicuity. On the one hand he advocates fighting to maintain the right of the Muslim to live by *Sharia* law and defend the honour of Islam. Yet, on the other, he does not differentiate between defensive and offensive jihad in his justification of the establishment of the House of Islam (*Dar al-Islam*). How this 'self-defence' explains the expansion of Islam into non-Muslim territories and how this justifies *jihad* against the West is never properly clarified.

In addition, it would also have been helpful for Akbar to consider the place of intra-Muslim *jihad*. Consideration of sectarian *jihad* which continues to threaten the political stability of Islamic nations and revivalist *jihad* which rails against the nominalism and secularism infiltrating Muslim communities, would have given further breadth to a subject which as Akbar's sub-title suggests is unfortunately restricted to the conflict with Christianity.

I suspect that with the West still living under the shadow of 9/11 and 7/7, *The Shade of Swords* will only serve to perpetuate a turbulent past into a turbulent future. I also suspect that those who read it will not read Firestone's book at all.

Andrew Buttress
Director of Spectrum Contemporary Christian Studies, UK
Postgraduate student London School of Theology

The Emergence of Islam

GABRIEL SAID REYNOLDS *The Emergence of Islam: Classical Traditions in Contemporary Perspective,* Fortress Press, 2012

Gabriel Said Reynolds' *The Emergence of Islam: Classical Traditions in Contemporary Perspective* (Fortress Press: 2012) is a masterfully written book. The argument is propelled by an engaging style, economy of words, and a momentum built in to the structure of the book. Reynolds' approach is academic and empirical, but the target audience is educated *non-specialists.* His tone is candid without being sensational or polemical. In fact, his ability to give context and a fair hearing to a wide spread of data is rather refreshing given the contentious nature of much writing on Muhammad and Islam. In terms of spirit one might place Reynolds somewhere between the poles of philo-Islamic advocates and anti-Islamic polemicists, a polarity which he explicitly illustrates with reference to Karen Armstrong and to Robert Spencer (locations 198-212, Kindle Edition).

In his book Reynolds has set out to address two inter-related questions. 1. What can we know about the emergence of Islam in history? and (secondarily) 2. How do Muslims see their own *ur*-history (location 4793, Kindle Edition)? The feast our author offers gives us some sense of the essential message of the Qur'an, the traditional history of the prophet and the early community, and the place of Islam in Muslim societies today.

Emergence proceeds in three parts. With a little critical evaluation included, Part One is primarily a presentation of the traditional Muslim view of the descent of the Qur'an and the flourishing of Muhammad as a prophet in seventh century Arabia. The narrative continues through the careers of the first four caliphs (to 661 CE). The meat of Reynolds' argument is served up in the "second course" (Part Two) which turns the tables on the classic method of interpreting the Qur'an via prophetic biography (*sira*) and *hadith*. Concluding that the *siras*, *hadiths*, and Qur'an commentaries were largely late constructions to explain a much earlier and partially inscrutable Qur'an, Reynolds seeks to examine the Qur'an's message without recourse to these usual historical props. Indeed, instead of using the Muslim historical sources to understand an early seventh-century Qur'an and its prophet, in Part Two he asks the Qur'anic text what it can reveal to us about the "real" early history of Islam. Finally, Part Three explores contemporary expressions of Islam and the perception and impact of the prophet and the classic texts on Muslim life, society, and politics. The enmeshed and complex interplay of Islam and modernity is fleshed out with interesting sketches of the evolution of an Islamic polity in Pakistan and of the explosion of the 1979 Iranian Revolution onto the world scene.

Reynolds' account of the standard story of the rise of Muhammad (in Meccan and Medinan phases) and of the early caliphate captures one's interest and covers extensive material elegantly and succinctly. Through both Parts One and Two the reader will glean a very fair sense of the narrative of Muhammad and the essentials of the Qur'an's message. Notably, Reynolds provides balanced coverage of both the Shi'i and Sunni construals of Islamic origins. Nonetheless, the plot really thickens when Reynolds presents his own historical perspective on the rise of Islam.

For Reynolds, the Qur'an itself is (almost) our only truly ancient contemporary source-text for the story of Muslim origins. The reader will have gleaned by now that for Reynolds the prophetic traditions, the *sira*-biography, and the august medieval commentators are not an accurate guide to the story of Muhammad and his mission. For him, these "historical" sources are mostly exegesis in the guise of history. The range of reasons for skepticism include the lateness of the traditional sources; the paucity of contemporaneous non-Muslim sources on Muhammad; the complete lack of any non-Islamic historical reference to Mecca as a pagan trade centre; anachronistic theo-political tendencies and contradictions in *hadiths*; dubious tendencies in the evolution of *isnad* patterns; and the befuddlement of the standard commentators over fundamental issues in the Qur'an, issues which should have been abundantly clear to anyone with access to genuine contemporary testimony (chapter five).

Many of the above arguments are familiar from the traditionalist-revisionist debates over Islamic origins. For me, Reynolds is at his most compelling when he turns to evidence from the Qur'an itself, set against a tableau of the late antique Middle East and the history of Eastern Christianity. With artful brevity he paints a picture of the early development of theology in the Christian East (including among the Arabs). In chapter seven Reynolds outlines what he describes as two theological styles running as an undercurrent in early Christian theology: *God as immanent* (Alexandria) over against *God as transcendent* (Antioch). Through the christological controversies these tensions were to eventuate in **three** ecclesial streams in the East, the Monophysite, Nestorian, and Melkite.

It is against this sectarian backdrop that the Qur'an comes into sharp relief (chapters 5-7). In essence, its preaching represents a **fourth**, competing, *Arab* stream, and one emphatically "transcendent" in theological vision. Enter here:

- once again, the evidence, or lack thereof, for a robust Meccan paganism in the non-Muslim historical records

- the fairly elusive presence of truly pagan interlocutors in the Qur'anic text[1]

- a heavily transcendent, monistic, and anti-incarnational theology in the text

- the marked evidence of christological controversy throughout the text

- the disproportion of this christological controversy in the text against the relative scarcity of Christians in the standard Islamic picture of Muhammad's Arabia

- the historical evidence of the Christianization of Arab populations from at least the fifth century (but lacking an Arabic Bible!)

- the frequent Qur'anic allusion to (orally based?) biblical story and legend (e.g., the Protoevangelium of James)

...and so on. It appears that the Qur'an emerges in an ethos of inter-confessional monotheistic contest, not so much in the pagan setting of Muslim tradition. Reynolds highlights Qur'anic themes such as its aggressive claim to Abraham through Ishmael [Q 2.127-129] and its emphasis on its Arabic character [Q 12.2; 26.192-195; 42.7]. The Qur'an's frequent reference to biblical tropes and its christological criticism are also important. Thus, this scripture is seen as the voice of a dynamic and ultimately successful movement which claimed a rooting in biblical salvation-history and which sought to overturn competing "biblical" traditions. This text is claiming, at long last, a holy status *for the Arabs* before the One God.

---

[1] In chapter five Reynolds discusses the "exceptional" appearance of what are traditionally seen as pagan goddesses in Sura 53.

Can Reynolds' reconstruction carry the day? Well, no one, including Reynolds himself, is anticipating upending the retrospective vision held dear throughout the Muslim world. We might also add that there certainly remain plenty of scholarly advocates for the reliability of the Islamic historical tradition. Further, our author's proposals entail some inherent modesty –they are suggestive not definitive. As Reynolds readily admits, in denying ourselves the detail, imagination, and theological agenda of the standard Islamic histories, we must be prepared to accept a less precise and less florid picture of the rise of early Islam (conclusion to Part Two). Still, relying mainly on the Qur'an as our historical source, the canvas is *not* blank. The lines of evidence cited above do *seem* to situate early Islam in the sectarian contest of the Middle Eastern monotheists *right from the start*. Arab paganism is not necessarily the central backdrop.

Naturally, several lines of inquiry would need to be pursued in ruling out a pagan context for various Qur'anic verses. Of course there are the clear occasions in which idol worship is in view in the recitation of *biblical* and extra-biblical tales about Abraham and others. Then there are the slightly more ambiguous passages, such as Q 2.165-166; 5.82 (Christians as distinct from "those who associate"); 6.22-23; 7.190f. These and many other passages need careful examination in determining the historical backdrop to be pagan or otherwise. Nonetheless, there is an intuitive plausibility to Reynolds' key move, to read the Qur'an in fruitful if sometimes tense conversation with the larger Biblical tradition, canonical and non, Jewish, and especially Christian. On these terms, Reynolds presents a fresh approach to the Muslim Scripture, one which beckons to further discovery.

A very real strength of Reynolds' work is his competence in the fields of Islamics, Middle Eastern antiquity, and the relevant languages, alongside his evident skill in communicating to the "average" educated reader. This work would serve quite well as an introductory text to Islam; *even without the critical reevaluation of Islamic origins*, the book is a readable presentation of the basic story of Muhammad and his scripture. And the benefits do not stop there. The third part of the book provides a very tactile introduction to the practice and impact of Islam in modern societies such as Pakistan, Saudi Arabia, Iran, and others. We are treated to a revealing look at the aggressive response of Islam to Western culture and paradigms, revealing both hostility and also assimilation in the interaction.

The book is nicely arranged so that in tandem with the author's argument the reader enjoys the added value of sidebars, photos, selected excerpts in translation, key personality profiles, etc. Textual artifacts include samples of Islamic constitutions and speeches, translations of various modern *fatwas* or ancient *hadiths* and so on. Along the way we glean bits of information ranging from legal regulations governing yawning during the prayers to mention of the prophet's penchant for toothpicks. We trace Pakistani models of Islam from an earlier openness and pluralism to the current scene with its use and abuse of the notorious blasphemy laws (chapter eight). We hear from voices as diverse as Ayatollah Khomeini and Samuel Zwemer and Naguib Mahfouz. This book is remarkable for its clarity, concision, and comprehensiveness.

Brent Neely
Nazareth Evangelical Theological Seminary
Israel

Khomeini's Ghost

CON COUGHLIN. **Khomeini's Ghost**. London Pan Books, 2009
ISBN 978-0-230-71455-7

Khomeini's Ghost, on the one hand, is an eloquent expression of concerns, fears and all that is, according to the Western mind, wrong with Iran's nuclear ambitions, but on the other, it is a powerful explanation of what may be, according to the Iranian mind, their legitimate right as a logical consequence of the struggles and sacrifices leading to and following Khomeini's Revolution of February 1979. Even today his legacy endures without any loss of power and its effects continue to be felt in the Middle East, America and indeed around the world.

Historically, Persia has always been a significant player on the world stage. She defeated the great Babylonian empire, served as a gateway to India for the British, and became crucial to the world's power balance after Russia's Bolshevik revolution of 1917. However, under the Shah even though by the 1960s Tehran had become more equal to Washington as America's dependence on Iran's oil increased, her unique identity as a religious civilization and as a government in touch with her people's values and aspirations had begun to wane.

Coughlin exposes how Khomeini first took on the cancer-ridden Shah ("a servant of the dollar" who in 1971 spent an estimated $100 million commemorating the capture of Babylon by Cyrus the Great in 539 BC), then the crumbling Iranian bureaucracy, followed by an opportunistic grab for media attention with the hostage taking of American embassy personnel. When the student activists demanded the exiled Shah in exchange, America found itself in a very difficult situation. After 444 days of a terrifying ordeal, fifty-two Americans did return home safely, but only after "The Great Satan" had been humiliated. The Carter administration's indecisiveness had played favourably for Khomeini, and his epoch-making revolution had once again put Iran on the centre stage of world politics. Of course, the nature of this centrality is a matter of perspective. Internationally, it led Iran to acquire immense importance and made her a state to reckon with among the community of nations.

Khomeini's story of mythical proportions begins with an orphan boy with an unusual name, Ruhollah, "the soul of God", who became the reviver of religious government in the contemporary world. He was steeped in Islamic scholarship and as a master orator gave some lasting slogans to the world. Throughout the book, the masterly narrator, Coughlin, very cleverly keeps Khomeini's charismatic personality and his radical Islamic ideology at the centre of a very fast-moving account which follows sixty-three year old Khomeini's exile from Iran to Najaff, the "Den of Snakes", in Iraq to France and back to Iran. His charismatic personality led some in Iran to identify themselves as "Khomeini Muslims", while others equated his flight from Paris to Tehran with the Prophet Muhammad's "flight" from Mecca to Medina in 622 AD.

Khomeini took on Iraq, led by the Sunni Baathist dictator Sadaam Hussein (who had grabbed power in 1968), but failed to win the Iran-Iraq War of 1980-88. After missing crucial opportunities when he could have called for a ceasefire while in a victorious position, Khomeini effectively conceded defeat to Iraq by accepting UN security resolution 598. Khomeini personally gave instructions for the acquisition of nuclear weapons for future warfare. (The reference to his letter on p. 242 mistakenly reads, "Iraq", instead of Iran.)

Victory or defeat: his people were unafraid to die, so powerful was his radical interpretation of their holy book. Young men and children willingly became cannon fodder when he introduced human wave attacks against Iraq. These attacks, launched by the *Basij,* an army of volunteers of 10-16 year-old boys and old unemployed men in their eighties who were deployed to clear the way for the real combatants to follow and fight, posed real challenges for Saddam's war machine.

The complex moves of power play of Iran's agents and agencies, both in the attention grabbing world news headlines as well as the blood chilling manoeuvres in the dark world of espionage, stemming from the aftermath of Khomeini's revolution is a continual theme throughout the book.

Other than America, Khomeini consistently denounced the existence of a Zionist state and his successor Khamenei called it "The cancerous tumour". Little surprise then, that Ahmadinejad, threatens to wipe it off the face of the earth. Ahmadinejad consistently reassures UN delegates that Iran does not have a (nuclear) weapon programme, and while in America stated that there are no homosexuals in Iran.

According to Coughlin, Tehran's involvement in Islamic terrorism has been well-established, both in Iran and around the globe, through the activities of Revolutionary Guards, Hamas, and Hezbollah. The authors of 9/11 commission report concluded a strong evidence of Iran's involvement in helping the attackers prior to the atrocity. And after the fall of Saddam Hussein, the Americans and the British had to contend with the Iranian back militias in Iraq.

Shah's anti-clerical drive, openly secular agenda, the role of SAVAK, his all-pervasive intelligence service infiltrating all aspects of Iran's society, combined with his close ties with America alienated a large segment of society from him. Khomeini decried the SAVAK but in time the Revolutionary Guards, started as a motley collection of Islamic fanatics brought together to defend the 1979 revolution, would become just as all pervasive taking his ideology to Iraq, Lebanon and other parts of the Islamic world. Iran's relentless campaign of intimidation against the state of Israel by supporting Hamas, the radical Palestinian Islamic group, is well documented by the author. It is also claimed that when Hamas came to power, Iran became its main financial backer and that in 2008 80% of Hizbollah's funding came from Iran. There were also clear indications that Iran was somehow involved in the Lockerbie bombings, but was let off lightly due to a dearth of concrete evidence. When President Bush made overt gestures of some sort of reconciliation towards Iran in 1989, Khomeini's response to the West appeared in the form of a *fatwa* on Salman Rushdie, the Indian born-Muslim writer of the infamous *Satanic Verses*. Theologically the book also offers interesting insights into the Shiaiism versus Suniism, the two major sects of Islam.

Khomeini had a vision, shared by others like Mohammed al-Sadr, of creating a universal Islamic state. He published his views in a slim volume, *Velayat-e Fiqah,* the "regency of the theologian". This, his radical philosophy of applying strict interpretation of Sharia law, later became known as Islamic fundamentalism.

Khomeini's Ghost reads like a historical novel and a political analysis at the same time. It is a fast moving narrative spanning nearly six decades of Iran's eventful history and is a testament to Coughlin's long term interest and therefore deep insights into her political psyche.

For those wanting to understand the psychological basis of Iran's unwillingness to give up its relentless pursuit of nuclear weapons this book is an excellent read, a masterly narrative packed with facts, and richly studded with fluent cross references. It offers insights into her current role on the world stage of power play. Khomeini, undoubtedly one of the most influential ideologues of the twentieth century, dreamed of an Iran with nuclear capabilities. His philosophy and strategy matters in the current world of politics and Iran's actions resulting from his legacy keep making headlines for many newspaper editorials around the world. Khomeini has gone but his ghost refuses to do so.

Dr Akhtar Injeeli
UK-based independent scholar researching the interaction between Islam and the West

Modern Muslim Identities

GERHARD HOFFSTAEDTER. *Modern Muslim Identities: Negotiating Religion and Ethnicity in Malaysia*. Copenhagen: NIAS Press, 2011. Xv + 272 pp. ISBN 978-87-7694-081-2.

This work begins with a striking assertion about the current state of play in Malaysia: "a Malay elite is maintaining a hegemonic system of control and cultural dominance, whilst juggling incursions into its political sphere by Islamic and Malay supremacists on the one hand and moderate civil society groups on the other." (vii)

Hoffstaedter formed the above views on the basis of an extended period of ethnographic research in various Malaysian locations, especially Selangor and Kelantan. He has shaped his arguments into seven main chapters.

Chapter One sets the scene in a most effective manner. The author provides a useful and accessible theoretical discussion of identity, stating from the outset that "in Malaysia ... racial identity is a key identity marker." (2) He is at pains to stress the role of elites in this identity formation, distinguishing between secular and Islamic elite, each of which has a powerful role to play. He foreshadows later discussion by declaring that "the Malaysian social contract guarantees the superiority of the Malays" (25), reinforcing this statement by adding that "the social contract provided the foundations for a system of governance based on inequality and exclusion." By this early stage the reader can be in no doubt that the author is committed to asking any question and reaching any conclusion, regardless of political sensitivities.

Chapter Two begins with a very helpful paragraph in which the author interacts with his friend Faris. This device, used to launch each chapter, serves to keep the discussion grounded and reminds readers that the focus is on real people, not theoretical constructs. Hoffstaedter surveys the historical factors leading to Malay and Muslim identities being conflated. He points out that the Malaysian Constitution defined Malay as agama/religion + bahasa/language + adat/customary law but in the early 21st century the latter two identity markers have declined in importance, leaving agama as the key marker.

He then introduces his notion of Islamicity, defining it as "the personification of Islamic space, the embedding of an all-encompassing worldview into personal belief..." (45) He returns to this in more detail later, finishing this excellent chapter by presenting the popular self-perception among Malays that they are "privileged as Malays by the Malaysian state and privileged as Muslims by God." (54)

The author devotes the third chapter to "an interrogation of the public space in Malaysia and what role race and religion, i.e. Malayness and Islam, play in it." (60) He observes that politics and the state are key actors in conceiving and shaping Islamic space in Malaysia. He points to the new administrative capital of Putrajaya, established in 1995 as the brainchild of Prime Minister Mahathir and filled with Islamic architecture.

But such state-shaping of Islamic identity is not restricted to the Federal Government. In 2005 the Islamic Party of Malaysia Government in the state of Kelantan declared its capital Kota Bharu to be "an Islamic City", in the wake of many years of Islamic legislation establishing Islamic practice as normative for the Kelantanese. Hoffstaedter observes that "the elite fashion a 'real' Islam or authoritative Islam, which is nonetheless internally contested." (73)

As part of the impact of state shaping religious identity and perceptions, the author refers to the policing of Islamic deviance (73ff) as well as ongoing debates surrounding supposed large scale conversions of Muslims to Christianity which emerged from rumour mongering reinforced by loose talk by government officials.

In Chapter Four the author considers former Prime Minister Abdullah Badawi's Islam Hadhari (progressive, civilizational Islam), and its role in engineering Malay Muslim identities. This set of principles represents Badawi's reconceptualization of the 624AD Constitution of Medina, aiming for inclusivism in a pluralist society. However, rising Islamist groups such as *Front Bertindak Anti Murtad* and *Pembela Islam* spoke with a contrary voice. Hoffstaedter concludes that Islam Hadhari has largely failed "because it runs counter to both progressive and conservative elements in civil society" (89) and did not connect with ordinary Malaysians.

In Chapter Five the author moves from a focus on government actors to a consideration of "civil society actors who are manipulating, resisting and influencing the state's control over

Islamicity, Islamic space and Malayness." (111) He observes that civil society, like the state, is another contested space in Malaysia where Malayness and Islam are fought-over concepts. He clarifies who he means by observing that "Civil society is as much the pro-democracy organisations and NGOs working for better working and living conditions, as it is the various fundamentalist movements, often proclaiming similar ends, but with radically different means." (113)

The groups who receive specific attention include progressive civil Islam groups, such as the Middle East Graduate Centre and Sisters in Islam, as well as reactionary civil society groups: FORKAD (Action front against apostasy), BADAI (Coalition against the Inter-Faith Commission), TERAS (Malay empowerment movement), and the Muslim Brothers, set up as a counterpoint to Sisters in Islam.

Chapter Six continues the discussion of civil society, turning its attention to a diverse set of themes, including spiritual places and spirit mediums. The author also considers the impact of online media in shaping Islamic identity, taking account of elements as current as Islamic applications on mobile phones. He observes that "the Islam on offer on the internet is global Islam ... [that] has been purified of ethnic and national cultures." (154) He devotes particular attention to the Tablighi Jamaat, a worldwide Islamic revivalist movement that is active in Malaysia.

In Chapter Seven the author draws the threads of preceding discussion together. He begins by asserting that state policies perpetuate fractured identity, divided along racial and religious lines. His friend Faris laments: "Although we're all truly Malaysian, it seems it is deemed that some are more Malaysian than others." (189)

Hoffstaedter holds both elites and elements of civil society responsible. The elites, he asserts, are the agents of "a system of exclusion and othering over time that culminates in a form of politicide against its main constituents, the Malays." (190) He defines politicide as state-sponsored and state-enacted notion of exclusion, reinforced by parts of civil society. He considers various modes of exclusion: mosques (the author was ejected from mosques on several occasions); Hari Raya Korban/Haji (the author was not allowed to eat meat from the sacrificed animal as he was not a Muslim); open houses (when Islamic feast days coincide with other faiths feast days, the tradition of sharing open houses is being increasingly challenged by certain conservative Islamic groups); Putrajaya (the author was denied access to a government department because he was wearing baggy shorts that were deemed unIslamic by security guards); halal eating places (at meal times people split into religious groups).

The author concludes the chapter by observing an irony: "the majority of Malays are not the 'beneficiaries of privilege.' In fact ... they are the most heavily policed and politicided." (219)

This book is a must-read for anyone interested in a variety of topics: Malaysia, multiculturalism and pluralism, Islam and modern society and so forth. Hoffstaedter is fearless in his assessment, which paints a none-too-rosy picture of the Malaysian state and elites. But his tone is never hysterical; rather it is reasoned, logical and powerful in its argumentation. His writing style is very accessible, with scholarly observations interspersed with slice of life insights that holds the attention of the reader. Having carried his reader on a coherent and well-constructed journey, Hoffstaedter ends with a recommendation for Malaysian authorities and elites, one that bears careful thought:

> "The first step must be an end to all forms of politicide against the majority and the minorities, in order to free the individual from the tyranny of racial-cum-religious politics and return agency to the individual. This includes allowing all individuals, especially Malays, to choose their religion." (227)

Dr Peter Riddell

Short reviews of new books on Islam in South and Southeast Asia

Articulating Islam: Anthropological Approaches to Muslim Worlds
Marsden, Magnus; Retsikas, Konstantinos (Eds.)
Dordrecht: Springer, 2013, ISBN 978-94-007-4267-3

This collection of arresting and innovative chapters applies the techniques of anthropology in analyzing the role played by Islam in the social lives of the world's Muslims. The volume begins with an introduction that sets out a powerful case for a fresh approach to this kind of research, exhorting anthropologists to pause and reflect on when Islam is, and is not, a central feature of their informants' life-worlds and identities. The chapters that follow are written by scholars with long-term, specialist research experience in Muslim societies ranging from Kenya to Pakistan and from Yemen to China: thus they explore and compare Islam's social significance in a variety of settings that are not confined to the Middle East or South Asia alone. The authors assess how helpful current anthropological research is in shedding light on Islam's relationship to contemporary societies. Collectively, the contributors deploy both theoretical and ethnographic analysis of key developments in the anthropology of Islam over the last 30 years, even as they extrapolate their findings to address wider debates over the anthropology of world religions more generally. Crucially, they also tackle the thorny question of how, in the current political context, anthropologists might continue conducting sensitive and nuanced work with Muslim communities. Finally, an afterword by a scholar of Christianity explores the conceptual parallels between the book's key themes and the anthropology of world religions in a broader context. This volume has key contemporary relevance: for example, its conclusions on the fluidity of people's relations with Islam will provide an important counterpoint to many commonly held assumptions about the incontestability of Islam in the public sphere.

*****

Muslim Minorities and Citizenship: Authority, Islamic Communities and Shari'a Law
Sean Oliver-Dee
Tauris Academic Studies, 2012, ISBN: 978-1-84885-388-1

The issues of citizenship, identity, and cohesion have rarely been as vital as they are today. Since the events of 9/11 and subsequent terrorist episodes in Bali, Madrid, London, and elsewhere, focus in this area has centered primarily upon Muslim minority communities living in the West. This book examines the question of citizenship and loyalty, drawing on the historical contexts of Muslim minorities living under British and French imperial rule in the nineteenth and twentieth centuries, and looks at how shari'a functioned within the context of imperial civil code. It draws important comparisons that are of immense relevance today, and engages with current debates about the compatibility of Islamic law with civil law in non-Islamic societies. Engaging with both Muslim minority and government perspectives, this is important reading for scholars, students, commentators, and policy-makers concerned with the question of Western engagement with its own minorities.

*****

Woman, Man, and God in Modern Islam
Theodore Friend
Grand Rapids & Cambridge: Eerdmans, 2011, ISBN: 978-0802866738

Award-winning historian Theodore Friend recently set out alone across Asia and the Middle East on a quest to understand firsthand the life situations of women in Indonesia, Pakistan, Saudi Arabia, Iran, and Turkey. Woman, Man, and God in Modern Islam recounts Friend's remarkable journey and relates hundreds of encounters and conversations with people he met along the way. Commingling a deep respect for Islam and his faith in the potential of women to change their worlds, Friend presents an open, exploratory outsider's perspective on women in five very different Islamic cultures -- timely fare for all who wish to broaden their world horizons.

*****

The Makings of Indonesian Islam: Orientalism and the Narration of a Sufi Past
Michael Laffan
Princeton: Princeton University Press, 2011, ISBN: 9780691145303

Indonesian Islam is often portrayed as being intrinsically moderate by virtue of the role that mystical Sufism played in shaping its traditions. According to Western observers--from Dutch colonial administrators and orientalist scholars to modern anthropologists such as the late Clifford Geertz--Indonesia's peaceful interpretation of Islam has been perpetually under threat from outside by more violent, intolerant Islamic traditions that were originally imposed by conquering Arab armies.

The Makings of Indonesian Islam challenges this widely accepted narrative, offering a more balanced assessment of the intellectual and cultural history of the most populous Muslim nation on Earth. Michael Laffan traces how the popular image of Indonesian Islam was shaped by encounters between colonial Dutch scholars and reformist Islamic thinkers. He shows how Dutch religious preoccupations sometimes echoed Muslim concerns about the relationship between faith and the state, and how Dutch-Islamic discourse throughout the long centuries of European colonialism helped give rise to Indonesia's distinctive national and religious culture.

The Makings of Indonesian Islam presents Islamic and colonial history as an integrated whole, revealing the ways our understanding of Indonesian Islam, both past and present, came to be.

*****

Varieties of Religious Authority: Changes and Challenges in 20th Century Indonesian Islam
Edited by Azyumardi Azra, Kees van Dijk, Nico J.G. Kaptein
Singapore: Institute of Southeast Asian Studies, 2010, ISBN: 9789812309402

The twentieth century was a fascinating period of profound political, social and economic changes in Indonesia. These changes contributed to the diversification of the religious landscape and as a result, religious authority was redistributed over an increasing number of actors. Although many Muslims in Indonesia continued to regard the ulama, the traditional religious scholars, as the principal source of religious guidance, religious authority has become more diffused and differentiated over time. The present book consists of contributions which all deal with the multi-facetted and multidimensional topic of religious authority and aim to complement each other. Most papers deal with Indonesia, but two dealing with other countries have been included in order to add a comparative dimension. Amongst the topics dealt with are the different and changing roles of the ulama, the rise and role of Muslim organizations, developments within Islamic education, like the madrasa, and the spread of Salafi ideas in contemporary Indonesia.

*****

Islamization and Activism in Malaysia
Julian C H Lee
Singapore: Institute of Southeast Asian Studies, 2010, ISBN: 978-983-3782-96-3

Islamization and Activism in Malaysia examines aspects of the increasing political and social profile of Islam in Malaysia and describes how different kinds of activists in Malaysia have sought to protect fundamental liberties and to improve the state of democracy in Malaysia. In particular, focus is paid to activists who engage with electoral process, the law and the public sphere, and in particular, to movements that cut across or combine these realms of action. Spanning the period of the Prime Ministership of Abdullah Badawi, Julian C. H. Lee's grounded analysis examines the most important issues of that period including the freedom of religion case of Lina Joy, the Islamic state debate, and events surrounding the 8 March 2008 general elections.

*****

Muslim Merit-making in Thailand's Far-South
Christopher M. Joll
Dordrecht: Springer, 2012, ISBN 978-94-007-2485-3

This volume provides an ethnographic description of Muslim merit-making rhetoric, rituals and rationales in Thailand's Malay far-south. This study is situated in Cabetigo, one of Pattani's oldest and most important Malay communities that has been subjected to a range of Thai and Islamic influences over the last hundred years. The volume describes religious rhetoric related to merit-making being conducted in both Thai and Malay, that the spiritual currency of merit is generated through the performance of locally occurring Malay adat, and globally normative amal 'ibadat. Concerning the rationale for merit-making, merit-makers are motivated by both a desire to ensure their own comfort in the grave and personal vindication at judgment, as well as to transfer merit for those already in the grave, who are known to the merit-maker. While the rhetoric elements of Muslim merit-making reveal Thai influence, its ritual elements confirm the local impact of reformist activism.

CSIOF News and Activities

Postgraduate Research Seminars on Islam and Related Topics 2012

Dhikr
Dr Moyra Dale, 17 April

Observations on the earliest list of alleged prophecies about Muhammad in the Bible
Denis Savelyev, 17 April

The Gentle Answer: a Christian-Muslim apologetics project
Dr Gordon Nickel, 22 May

The Holy Spirit in the Qu'ran
Dr Mark Durie, 22 May

The first Protestants in the Arab world: a startling case of historical amnesia
Rev. Andrew Lake, 22 May

Church and Mosque in Sub-Saharan Africa
Dr Peter Riddell, 18 August

Islam south of the Sahara – Somalia and Kenya
Ken Okello, 18 August

Mali and Nigeria: Islam at the Gate
Elizabeth Kendal, 18 August

Jihad and Old Testament wars – Are they the same?
Dr Bernie Power, 21 August

A Christian socio-political response to injustice and oppression resulting from Pakistan's blasphemy laws
Rev. Qaisar Julius, 23 October

The Life, Work & Legacy of Carl Pfander, 19th Century Apologist to Islam
Rev. Jay Smith, 23 October

Glossary

Term	Description
Caliph	The successor to Muhammad as political and military ruler of the Islamic community
Dar al-Islam	The House of Islam; areas where Islam has political dominance
Dar al-Harb	The House of War; the rest of the world not under Islam
Da'wa	Mission
Dhimmi	"protected" non-Muslim communities living under Islamic rule
Durura	Necessity
Fasiq	Sinner
Hadith	Authorative traditions of all that Muhammad said and did
Hajj	Pilgrimage (to Mecca)
Hijra	Migration
Huda	Guidance
Ijtihad	Process of legal deduction by which a scholar produces a legal opinion
Imam	(Sunni meaning) leader of congregational prayer in mosque (Shia meaning) leader of all the faithful, all of the Shia
Jahiliyya	Paganism/ Ignorance
Jihad Jehad	Holy war; "a continuous and never-ending struggle waged on all fronts including political, economic, social, psychological, domestic, moral and spiritual." [Malite ,p54]
Jinn	Demon/ spiritual being

Term	Description
Jizya	Poll taxfor non-Muslims living under Islamic rule
Kafir	Unbeliever/ disbeliever/ infidel
Maslaha	Public good
Mujaddid	Renewer of Islam
Mujahiddin	Holy warriors
Mu'min	Believer
Nur	Light
Saracens	Term Christians used for Muslims in early Islamic period
Seerah	Biography of Muhammad
Shahada	Creed: "There is no God but God and Muhammad is his messenger
Sunna	Way or example of Muhammad
Sura	Chapter of the Qur'an
Tafsirs	Qur'anic commentaries
Tahrif	Corruption, distortion (of text)
Taqlid	Imitation of judgements made by earlier scholars
Tawhid	Oneness of Allah (Sufi meaning) Oneness with Allah
Umma	One Muslim community worldwide
Zakat	Almsgiving at the mosque (Sufi meaning) totally giving oneself to Allah and to a Sufi brotherhood

Notes for Contributors

Submission requirements:

Manuscript

(1) Papers should not exceed 2000 words, although the Editor retains the discretion to publish papers beyond this length.

It is preferable that submissions be prepared in Microsoft Word format.

All papers are to be written in English, and an English transliteration given to any quotations or short phrases in original language.

Authors are advised to use gender inclusive and non-discriminatory language.

Any visuals should be integrated into the document, or sent separately as separate jpg or gif files with an explanation as to their position in the paper.

Footnotes and bibliography should follow the style used in previous issues of the Bulletin.

Submission

(2) Papers to be considered for inclusion are to be submitted directly to the Editor.

Submissions are to be forwarded via electronic mail to csiof@mst.edu.au. If submitting within Australia, a hard copy must also be posted to CSIOF, PO Box 6257 Vermont Sth, Vic 3133.

A declaration that the submitted articles are your own work and that you've acknowledged the work/s of others used in the articles in the references, etc. must be included with any submission.

A covering letter that includes the authors' names, titles, affiliations, with complete mailing addresses, including email, telephone and facsimile numbers should be attached to the paper.

Review of Submissions

(3) All submissions will be sent to referees for anonymous recommendation.

The Editor holds the right to make editorial corrections to accepted submissions.

Copyright

The CSIOF Bulletin is published by the Melbourne School of Theology Press. The copyright for any published papers will remain with the author. MST publishes these papers on the following conditions:

- They do not appear elsewhere (including web pages) for 180 days from the date of publication in the CSIOF Bulletin.
- Whenever they are printed elsewhere (including web pages), the following notice will be included: "This article first appeared in the __ issue of the *CSIOF Bulletin* series".
- We retain the right to use the paper in any CSIOF publications, reprints, or in electronic form (ie. Online, CD-Rom, etc.).
- We retain the right to use a portion or description of the paper with your name in our promotional material.
- Authors are themselves responsible for obtaining permission to reproduce copyright material from other sources.
- The author will be presented with one copy of the publication.

Disclaimer

The opinions and conclusions published in the CSIOF Bulletin series are those of the authors and do not necessarily represent the views of the Editor or the CSIOF. The Occasional Papers serve purely as an information medium, to inform interested parties of religious trends, discussion and debates. The Occasional Papers do not intend in any way to actively promote hatred of any religion or its followers.

www.ingramcontent.com/pod-product-compliance
Lightning Source LLC
Chambersburg PA
CBHW072150020426
42334CB00018B/1943